More praise for *How Can We Keep from Singing*

"With an ear for the music of language as well as for the nuances of pitch and meter, Goldsmith's passion for singing becomes tangible. Her words soar, growl, cry and whisper. And they inspire."
—*Publishers Weekly* (starred review)

"There are insights for knowledgeable musicians and clear explanations for neophytes—a little history, a little theory, a little pedagogy, some soul-baring, and much humor. Singers will find themselves thinking, 'Yes that's it exactly,' as the author puts into words what is paradoxically shared with others in a public setting—the joy and spiritual nourishment that come from singing."
—*Library Journal*

"Be warned: by reading this book you abandon the idea that music is a cultural decoration at the edge of your days. *How Can We Keep from Singing* puts musical resonance where it belongs—at the core of your life, a current more jolting than electricity, a currency more global than money. Joan Oliver Goldsmith, your mercurial narrator, conducts you gracefully among the surprisingly connected worlds of commerce, music, and spiritual discovery, leaving you with a precious recognition: you need never live a divided life again. Music powers all."   —Kim Stafford, author
of *Having Everything Right*, director of the
Northwest Writing Institute at Lewis & Clark College

"[A] rousing book that salutes the passion, the joy, and the pleasures of singing, music, and practice. . . . This is a book to enjoy and share with your friends—especially those with a passion for music and the passionate life."
—*Spirituality and Health*

"Goldsmith has a large and long view of love. She knows that you don't always get what you want, but you can get some deeper understanding of yourself and other human beings while trying to get what you want."   —Robert Fulghum, auth
All I Really Need to Know I Learned

How Can We Keep from Singing

Music and the Passionate Life

by Joan Oliver Goldsmith

 W. W. Norton & Company   New York • London

Since this page cannot legibly accommodate all the copyright notices, page 13
constitutes an extension of the copyright page.

For information about permission to reproduce selections from this book,
write to Permissions, W. W. Norton & Company, Inc., 500 Fifth Avenue,
New York, NY 10110

The text of this book is composed in 9.5/15.5 Caxton Light with the display set in
Centaur Italic and Centaur Swash initial caps.
Composition by Sue Carlson
Manufacturing by Courier Westford
Book design by Dana Sloan
Production manager: Julia Druskin

Library of Congress Cataloging-in-Publication Data

Goldsmith, Joan Oliver.
How can we keep from singing : music and the passionate life /
by Joan Oliver Goldsmith.
p. cm.
ISBN 0-393-02024-X
1. Choral singing. 2. Choirs (Music) 3. Music, Influence of. 4. Music—Philosophy
and aesthetics. I. Title.

ML1500 .G65 2001

781'.11—dc21   2001030073

ISBN 0-393-32364-1 pbk.

W. W. Norton & Company, Inc., 500 Fifth Avenue, New York, N.Y. 10110
www.wwnorton.com

W. W. Norton & Company Ltd., Castle House,
75/76 Wells Street, London W1T 3QT

1 2 3 4 5 6 7 8 9 0

For Mom and Dad
and Dede

My life flows on in endless song
Above earth's lamentation.
I hear the real though far off song
That hails a new creation.
Through all the tumult and the strife
I hear the music ringing.
It sounds an echo in my soul.
How can I keep from singing!

—based on a nineteenth-century hymn

Contents

Gratitudes

When my aunt, Edith Oliver, died, I'd
been working on this book for many years, but I hadn't yet found
a publisher. Her legacies included the financial support needed to
complete the last three drafts, as well as the phrase "I'm so proud
of you," which rang in my ears even when the struggle filled me
with despair. All the words are for you, Dede.

The Minnesota Chorale has blessed and challenged me with
extraordinary musical experiences since 1987. I am deeply grateful to my fellow singers and to those who have led this enterprise
over the years: artistic director Kathy Saltzman Romey, her pred-
ecessor artistic director Joel Revzen, personnel director Barbara
Lundervold, accompanist Barbara Brooks, and executive director
Camille A. Kolles.

Scott Edelstein nurtured and coached me through the process
of finding a publisher. Nickie Dillon proofread, copyedited, and
prepared several drafts of the manuscript for submission, leaving
me free to deal with words rather than computers. W. W. Norton's
Alane Salierno Mason, editor and guardian angel of literature,
saw possiblities and problems invisible to others, and provoked
me into better writing. Editorial assistant Stefanie Diaz provided
invaluable support on administrative matters. David Stanford Burr
not only copyedited but also fact-checked the final manuscript,
saving me from a couple of really stupid errors. And Eve Tal in

Israel made the many telephone calls necessary to secure permission to quote "Shir LaShalom." Thank you all.

Thanks to writers and visionaries Julie Tallard Johnson, Shannon King, Laurel Reinhardt, Tamara Truer, and Anne Welsbacher for years of experience, support, hope, and good munchies at our monthly meetings. Also to Lonnie Bell, Lenore Franzen, Ellie Garrett, and Mary Jellison, whose strengths as artists and businesswomen fill me with wonder.

Thanks to my nonsinger readers: Steve Kaplan, who makes everyone around him shine brighter; Jim Romano, who wouldn't let me cut "thisness;" Pat Argyros, whose excitement always rekindled mine; and Tessa Bridal, a writer who combines extraordinary sensitivity with profound common sense.

Also to my singing readers, especially Sandra Davis, Liz Nordling, and Chris Trost, who so graciously let me include bits of their lives in my stories.

I owe much to my corporate clients who opened not only their budgets but their hearts to me, enabling me to see that the spiritual issues of music are to be found everywhere. Thanks especially to Jane Anderson, Anne Greer, Denny Nowlin, and Ron Wenaas.

My gratitude to music teachers has an essay all its own, but I am deeply indebted to writing teachers as well: Lawrence Sutin, who said "I think you have something there"; Janet Hagberg, who agreed; Myrna Kostash, who told me, "Write more about the music"; and Kim Stafford, who challenged "If it's not fun, why are you doing it?" My father, Robert Goldsmith, impressed upon me as soon as I could talk that words matter, that expressing ideas clearly is rarely easy but always worth doing. Thanks Dad.

My mother, Joyce Goldsmith, taught me a performer's discipline and joy, and has in my adult life become my greatest friend. My sisters, Diane and Vicki Goldsmith, provide unstinting friendship, love, and wisdom that gets me through good times and bad.

Thanks to Mort, Rita, and Emma Schlesinger for creating a loving space where good practicing happens and for making me laugh when I take myself too seriously.

And thanks, most of all, to music makers everywhere—whatever your instrument. Every note you sound nourishes the air we all breathe.

Credits

How Can We Keep from Singing

Overture: Playing the Invisible Instrument

When I make music, adventures happen. I sit at the feet of a grand old lady of spirituals, who tells stories of escaped slaves and Carnegie Hall recitals. I find myself on stage in Mexico City singing Mahler's glorious Symphony of a Thousand, while tenors stumble offstage to throw up in conveniently placed buckets. I am awed by the rich contributions made by the not famous—the fifteenth violinist, the accompanist, the singers in the chorus—the multitudes of voices who sing Beethoven's Ninth at Orchestra Hall, but never Mimì at the Met. We teach, drive school buses, write corporate brochures, whatever it takes—but we keep singing.

We're everywhere—the passionate, committed, talented, frequently unpaid or underpaid workers who make possible the great things of life. We're the utility infielder, the middle manager, the small-enterprise entrepreneur.

We are described by what we do, not by labels like professional or amateur. We work with craftsmanship and artistry. We create excellence. But for whatever reason—lack of luck, overweening ambition, the physiology that creates an operatic-size voice or Olympic athlete—we do not make it to the top.

We do not become CEOs of Fortune 500 companies. It's hard for us to believe we have significance as individuals. After all, when we get sick, the show goes on and the audience doesn't even notice. Yet collectively, we are indispensable and sometimes magnificent.

Without us, the CEO would not have a company nor the conductor an instrument. A lonely picture, that: the conductor dancing up there on the podium, waving his or her arms, reaching for sound and receiving none, because the not famous suddenly stopped.

We have a particular kind of courage—not the courage of those who climb mountains, but the courage of those who show up and practice. Not every day, perhaps, or even every year. We take time off to attend to loved ones or earn a living or indulge our exhaustion—but once that's accomplished, back we come. It puzzles and amazes me. The obvious rewards—money and recognition—aren't there, and the price is high. It would be so much less trouble to sit home and watch television.

The reason for this glorious insanity, it seems to me, has something to do with an invisible instrument we all carry inside —a creative spirit that must be expressed if the soul is not to die a slow, bleak death.

If you find yourself pulled beyond all practicality toward doing something—writing poetry, building a business, restoring old cars, planting a secret garden; if at four in the morning the

right word comes to you, the perfect flower to plant in that particular spot—you are playing your invisible instrument.

For me, the invisible instrument manifests through the voice,
that mysterious sound maker composed of vocal cords, lips,
tongue, breath, and spirit. It's a peculiar and fascinating instrument, a peculiar and fascinating life.

There is never enough time. It is harder than you ever imag-
ined. You are never as good as you want to be. And if tonight was
nearly perfect, watch out, because tomorrow you may slip up and
commit the chorister's greatest sin—singing an "unpaid solo."

Always, always they will ask you to give more—more concentration, more purity of sound, better line, finer adagio. They
will ask and you will ask it of yourself. You will especially ask
yourself what you are doing here after a hard day's work at your
day job, when you don't feel that good anyway, and your spouse
is mad at you, and your kids say you never get anything right,
and there isn't enough money to pay all of the bills. Then suddenly it flows—a bar, a phrase, perhaps even a whole movement—and you are the physical instrument of something higher.

Then you know again creation's assignment: to learn the
notes, to find your music. The invisible instrument is the one
instrument we must all learn to play.

A Box of
Sound Bites

Shh. Listen to the sounds that surround you. Notice the pitches, the volume, the timbre, the many lines of counterpoint. As light taught Monet how to paint, the earth may be teaching you music.

∾

HAVE YOU ever turned a pond into a kettledrum? I learned how from a grownup in Minneapolis, but it works equally well with a twelve-year-old in New York's Central Park. You find a pond that is starting to ice over. It mustn't be frozen solid. Then you find some comfortable rocks. They don't even have to be good skipping rocks. This is easier than skipping rocks. You just throw, underhand, overhand—it doesn't matter. *Boing-uh, boing-uh, boing-uh*, over the surface they bounce, reverberating through new ice and cold water. This seems particularly magical at dusk, but any time is fine.

You walk around the pond, seeing how many different pitches you can make. Thick ice: low pitches. Thin ice: high pitches. You attract envious attention from people too proper for this activity. Little dogs in little sweaters look at you quizzically.

∾

I HAVE this recurring daydream—that some morning I'll wake up, go to the door to let the cat out, and there, in the center of the doormat, surrounded by the jumble of shoes and boots, will be a pale blue velvet box. I'm not surprised to see it there, but I am surprised that it's blue, and not red. Boxes of chocolates are usually red, and that's what this looks like.

I let the cat out as planned, bring the box in, place it on the dining room table, and open it. The shapes in the paper cups are the shapes of chocolates—long and thin, round, square, crescent shaped like cashew nuts—but they are not the least bit chocolate colored. Yellow, green, pink, red, and blue—each with an odd luminosity.

I pop a blue one in my mouth: almost tasteless, perhaps slightly salty. The sound of ocean fills my ears. Waves gather seawater into themselves, crest, crash, then retreat. I hear the cries of a seagull as it soars close, then away. I know this beach. I remember the precious hours I have stolen away from family to walk Nauset—the first big-wave beach as one travels toward the tip of Cape Cod. In memory I walk the path from the parking lot through the dunes, feel the sun and wind on my face. The sights and feelings I know I am remembering. The sounds I actually hear.

I chew slowly, then not at all, letting whatever this thing is melt on my tongue. Slowly, slowly the morsel shrinks; the sounds become softer, until finally nothing.

I look into the box. More shapes, a rainbow of who-knows-what. And empty spaces. And I know, in this dream, that part of my job in life is to fill the box, to listen with full attention, so that a year from now, or fifty years from now, whatever my circumstances, I will be wealthy in sound bites.

∾

I'VE BEEN collecting sounds since I was little. My room on the second floor of the house on Senate Place seemed high up in the sky to me. Morning meant sunlight flowing like Joni Mitchell's butterscotch through the windows and birds squawking from the tree branches outside—jays, probably, or crows. A piquant mix, the warmth of the sun punctuated by the *Ak Ak* of strident birds.

Long before kindergarten, train sounds became friends. Dad took the Stamford Local to work every morning. In the evening Mom piled the three kids and the Labrador retriever into the (appropriately named) station wagon to pick him up. We'd wait with the anticipation of a Broadway audience before the star's entrance until—yes, there it was, off in the distance. The clackety-clack slowed. The train hissed to a stop, then commented *HUH*—for a job well done—and regurgitated Dad: evening newspaper, attaché case, suit, tie, and smile. We'd head home for cocktails—martinis for the grownups, raw vegetables and peanuts for everybody.

Then I got old enough—twelve—to take the train myself and that *HUH* meant we had arrived at Grand Central Station. All I had to do was walk the mica sparkly sidewalk to the tunnel entrance, where my aunt would take me by the hand and lead me to that most magical of experiences—a weekend in New York.

The sounds of morning at apartment 4D, on East 90th Street between Park and Lex: Saturday—crash, bang, rumble as the garbage men went about their business. They called to each other, little snippets of melody above the percussion, the phrases echoing in the space between buildings. Sundays all the church bells on earth congregated in Manhattan, I was sure of it, tolling in majestic monotony, playing hymns on the more nimble carillon. Years later, I knew Poe's poem the first time I read it—not the narrator's wild mania, but the repeated chorus: the bells, bells, bells, bells—seven times, verse after verse. I tasted the familiar ringing and the singing as tongue, lips, and teeth formed the words.

∽

I LIVE in a city, so I cannot see most of the stars most of the time. Orion cuts through on a clear winter's night, bless him, and often a bright planet will appear. I can watch the moon rise over the Mississippi River from my living room window, and I do. But, for the most part, I must listen for signs of heaven.

I mostly don't need an alarm clock. I have neighbors. Their footsteps thud gently overhead at 6:00 A.M. The floor squeaks, the toilet flushes. Then more footsteps. Then the gurgle of the coffeemaker and that best of all smells. A reminder of community, of who feeds the cat when I'm away, who got me to the emergency room when I fell and smashed up my face. Time to get up.

I also tell time by the Lake Street Bridge. It spans the Mississippi, joining Minneapolis to St. Paul just a block away. The cars go over in waves of hums—Mr. Doppler's effect—pitch rising when they're closer, descending as they zoom off. In the early hours, I can distinguish each car traveling toward or away from me. But as it gets closer to seven and then eight, when the people with serious jobs really must be on their way, the waves of hums combine to become one long baritone obbligato, punctuated by house finches and cardinals greeting the day outside my window.

A lifetime ago—or so it seems—the birds at the beach at Westport, Connecticut, saved my soul. Every day I walked to the job I hated as a legal secretary, walked the long way, the roundabout hour-and-a-quarter way. I did this for the pleasure of walking, placing one foot after the other in that steady rhythm that comforts both earth and traveler. But even more, I did it for the ten minutes of road along the beach. Gulls cried in my left ear; town birds twittered and chirped in my right. I didn't slow down. I needed those eight hours of typing and emptying out-baskets to pay debts from a failed business. But every day that crazy stereo of land and seabirds lightened my heart.

∾

IF YOU hold your nose, water coming from the kitchen tap sounds like bacon frying. Thus the illusory nature of sound without the other senses.

I once drove between walls of fire: fields of sugar cane burning on the island of Maui. Four o'clock on the road to dawn at Haleakala, the cratered House of the Sun. The strips of land adjacent to the road had been wetted down to keep the fire from spreading, but twenty feet away on either side and at least twenty feet high, yellow-red flames grasped at the sky. I closed my eyes. It could have been a waterfall, a big one like Niagara. No individual crackles like a fire in a fireplace, but a million high pitches, thirsty, rushing upward in a firefall.

The sounds of scuba diving are equally bizarre. All that costuming and rehearsal—mask, fins, oxygen tank, certification classes—and that glorious show—multicolored parrot fish, graceful angel fish feeding at a coral reef—only to hear munching (a sound like the crackle of Rice Krispies in a bowl of milk) over a background of heavy breathing.

∞

How USEFUL is this predilection for collecting sounds? Well, it certainly gets a person noticing noise. I live in a state where people are perfectly willing to accept the airport commission's solution to increasing air traffic: increase the insulation in homes near the airport. No matter that, as you walk around Lake Nokomis in the summertime, you can't converse for more than three minutes without having to stop and wait until the plane passes and you can hear the person next to you again.

But this is also the state in which, year after year, every time the referendum comes up, people who have never been to the BWCA, that tract of wilderness touching Canada, vote to keep it a Boundary Waters *Canoe* Area—no motorized boats allowed. Me, too. I want it waiting for me, quietly.

Leaf blowers really piss me off. If you have to wear hearing protectors to operate a machine, why should I be subjected to the noise? I have yet to see a leaf blower doing anything that would faze a rake or a broom, except maybe blow tree leaves out of bushes, which is, of course, an important contribution to neighborhood esthetics.

One person's noise is another's music. The sound of a Harley-Davidson motorcycle is so beautiful to some that the company fought for six years to trademark its roar.

∾

THE STAGE lights come up. Musicians walk on, a few at a time, tighten their bows, adjust their valves and start noodling—bits and pieces of what's to come, riffs of possibility. Then the concertmaster makes his entrance—or hers—and the oboe sounds an A—first for the strings, then for the winds. Four hundred forty vibrations per second made by horsehair pulled over catgut, and wooden tubes with vibrating reeds, and enormous copper kettles with animal skins stretched tight over them, and brass containers meant to be blown while adjusting valves and sliding tubes. Things of silver and brass and wood, things that are rubbed and beaten and blown, women and men, evening gowns and tuxedos, one note. The conductor strides to the podium, acknowledges applause, raises baton—and there, in that silent instant at the top of the beat, is all that can be said about portent and intention.

In my box of sound bites there are no jackhammers, no snowmobiles, no Jet Ski's, no children wailing. Music but no Muzak.

It's my box. Put what you want in yours.

How Can We Keep from Singing

*M*y new landlady kept the thermostat set low, but the real cold radiated from the rock of ice in my stomach. I would curl up tight in the single bed in my rented room—blankets piled high—and the fumes from the ice rock would seep out through my skin to fill the room with gray fog.

I don't know why I picked up the phone.

"Minnesota Chorale," said the voice at the other end.

My landlady's house had pale, hardwood floors; cross-stitched samplers on the walls amid pictures of blond, Norwegian-American children smiling fiercely at the camera; and a piano, out of tune, I could play if I liked, while she was at work.

"When are auditions?"

The receiver was slimy cold in my hand. I hadn't had a voice lesson in eight years. What the hell did I think I was doing? Oh, sure I had gone to a great music school, and taught singing, and voiced a few commercials in Minnesota. Then off to the Big Apple to break into the big time. It had taken New York only one year to send me fleeing into the business world.

From T-shirts to the silk blouses of sales and marketing: expense account dinners, presentations to Fortune 500 companies, quarterly numbers, company-sponsored tuition for my MBA. Instant respectability: mortgage bankers smiling. And an adrenaline rush just like performing, since everything in business is urgent all the time.

Eight years of no practicing. No lessons. No classes. Still I breathed and walked the earth. Astonishing.

Then I left my job to join the company my husband and I had started, and entered a nightmare of lies, infidelity, and near bankruptcy.

∞

"Usually auditions are in May," said the cheerful voice, "but we have a few openings now, so we'll be holding auditions week after next. You'll need one song in English, one in a foreign language, and you'll do some sight reading. Oh, and we're singing the Brahms *Requiem* at Orchestra Hall this Saturday. You might want to come."

So I heard the Brahms *German Requiem* for the first time not on a recording, but in a concert hall. Sitting alone in the mezzanine, I experienced the physicality of sound in a way electronics can never equal.

The slow, slow march of the second movement begins in a whispered unison, 150 voices each focusing immense energy into a laser beam of sound and sending it beyond the back row.

Denn alles Fleisch es ist wie Gras
(For all flesh is as grass)

The strings play the dragging beat of a funeral cortege: step hold hold, step hold hold.

und alle Herrlichkeit . . .
(And all the glories of humankind are as the flowers of the grass.)

Step hold hold. Again and again, orchestra and chorus mired in sorrow and tension, heaviness and pain.

Then this tiny sound explodes into a shout of rage. The same words unleashed into octaves at full fortissimo. The wall of sound slapped my face, moved through my skin, sinking into my belly, shaking me with a fury I didn't even know how to feel yet.

And then, when he has you—this agnostic composer who dared to write a requiem in his own language, choosing text that spoke to him rather than the Latin Catholic Mass—when he has you in his hand, feeling everything you've tried so hard not to feel because if you felt it all you'd shatter into a million pieces and you haven't got time for that now because you've got to survive. When you're open and raw, the balm comes, the lilting "*So seid nun geduldig, lieben Brüder.*" The 3/4 tempo of the funeral procession lightens and quickens: "Therefore be patient, dear brothers, until the coming of the Lord."

The cortege begins to dance.

He does this over and over for almost an hour, taking you through grief and comfort, fugue and majesty and waltz, until you are exhausted and clean.

I sat motionless, in a sea of thundering applause. He had felt this and said it, and I was changed.

∾

WHERE HAD "I" disappeared to all those years? "I" suited up and brought achievements home like a cat offering up a dead bird. But "we" did, "we" thought, "we" even felt. Who the hell was "I"? Evidently someone who needed music.

Rusty vocal cords? All right. Acute stage fright? Duly noted. I walked over to the piano, stood directly in front of middle C and took a deep breath. "Nnn" on a high note, sliding down, slowly, smearing through each pitch, tickling the nose, landing where it will. Now higher. Practice begins again.

If nothing else, singing reminds us that we are beings that vibrate and breathe. The opera singer's cliché, "me me me" and all those sliding glissandos on "nn," "mm," and "oo" are about one thing—turning a human body into a tube that produces a resonant, focused tone that can be heard at the back of the hall.

Strange that we talk so much about how it sounds and rarely about how good it feels, how natural: an extension of all those hums that occur in our language, small glissandos of meaning: "Mmm, I'll think about it." "Mmm, I don't know." "Mmm, delicious."

So. Begin with "mm" *and* "nn." *Now put the vowel in the same spot. I remember. Not so hard. Breathe in, resonate out. Go for the feeling, not the sound.* Others hear us through the vibrations of air. We hear ourselves also through the vibrations of our own body. Deceptive. *Trust the rest of the body, but not the ears.*

I imagine myself as a clarinet—not a clarinetist, but the instrument itself, straight up and down with just a bit of a flare at the bottom. I remember my older sister assembling her high school clarinet: starting with the flared bell, twisting each section of wooden tubing onto the next until it lined up just right, then putting the reed in her mouth to wet it, attaching reed to mouthpiece and topping off the whole. A clear channel for the air, no stress of kink or twist.

I love the clarinet's changeling nature, its versatility. The clarinet in Gershwin's *Rhapsody in Blue* opens with a low note, then a long squee-ee-eeze upward into a guffaw: Yuk, yuk, yuk, yuk, each laugh descending a half step. For Mozart's clarinet concerto, the instrument changes into a costume of velvet and lace to proffer elegant melodies. I love its mellow tone. When someone says the prayer of St. Francis: "Lord, make me an instrument of thy peace," I know the instrument is a clarinet. And I want to spell the word "piece."

I focus on keeping my body as stable and unconstricted as a clarinet. Lips, teeth, and tongue are just keys, valves to open and close as needed for consonants and vowels.

But something must supply air and energy to the system. During my eight nonsinging years, I breathed, of course. Deeply, I thought. I rode my bike. I swam. I stepped up and down a million steps getting nowhere in aerobics class. I sighed from time to time, as one does in this life: inhale slowly, raising the shoulders; release air and shoulders together. "HHaaaahhh." Exhalation, and some bit of tension is gone. I sampled yoga—breathe in for 8, hold for 4, breathe out for 8, hold for 4. But these rhythms are all wrong for a wind instrument, and the voice is certainly a wind instrument.

You breathe in—fast, deep, full—and then spin the breath out, carefully releasing it at just the right rate, like fishing line. Every once in a while the music gives you time for a slow inhalation and you use every morsel of it, gratefully. But whether you've got one beat or four, you breathe low first—filling belly and lower back—inflate under the lower ribs, then expand the chest without raising the shoulders. Raised shoulders can lead to neck tension. The lungs clearly do not reach the belly, but that's where it *feels* as if the breath starts—in singing, in yoga, in sleeping babies and animals. As near as I can figure, the diaphragm—that big floor of muscle under the lungs—pushes down to allow the lungs to expand, which pushes the guts and organs out of the way, which, in turn, expands the belly.

Do singers think about this each time we breathe? Of course not, any more than I think about the neural and muscular activity required for my hand to pick up a glass of water. I think about breathing from my belly. And about blowfish. Some people call them puffers. In an instant, these little guys can transform themselves from their normal slim fish shapes into round, taut balloons—just by inhaling air or water. They make it look so easy.

That's me: part clarinet, part blowfish.

It began to come back. Oh, not all of my vocal technique. Tone, flexibility, range, breath control would take two years to regain, not two weeks. But the pleasure of moving my particular body in the ways of a creature that vibrates and breathes.

∾

Singing, the first art.

Before we draw or dance or even crawl, we sing. We begin by making sounds with pitches attached. Some of our initial squeals and gurgles will become language, but some are on their way to becoming song. Robert Jourdain discusses this process (among many others) in his book *Music, the Brain, and Ecstasy*. At two months, "some infants can replicate the pitch and melodic contour of their mother's songs. . . . Between 12 and 18 months, just as babbling turns to discrete words, infants start to elongate vowels in a way that is clearly musical." (I have witnessed singing appearing before language: I baby-sat for a child who could not talk yet, but would join in perfectly on the "ee I ee I oh" refrain of "Old MacDonald Had a Farm.") As infants then toddlers, we babble, we sing snippets of songs, we make up snippets ourselves. Then by three or four we begin the serious business of duplicating the music we hear around us.

Just as *each* human being begins to sing early, so, it is surmised, did *all* human beings. Perhaps primitive humans sang, as composer Dominick Argento suggests, before speech—humming a child to sleep; wailing over the wounded body of a loved one; moaning in prayer to whatever makes the world what it is; crying out joyfully when life was good. The primal beginnings of the lullaby, the lament, the hymn, and the glee.

In the late 1980s, French archaeologists Iégor Reznikoff and Michel Dauvois tried something new as they explored the caves in southwestern France—they sang. Lo and behold, the chambers with the most paintings were also the most resonant. If the sophistication of the Cro-Magnon artwork can be taken as an indication, these caves may have been the sites of multimedia religious ceremonies, with singing accompanied by flutes, drums, and whistles.

∞

HUMAN BEINGS sing because we have to. When we're happy or sad or angry, energy builds up inside. Then, before the pressure can do damage, a valve opens and we cry or laugh or sing. And once those tears or notes are outside of us, the universe shifts a little. Tears dry cool on the cheek. Laughter infects those around us. And as for notes, well, "the blues is celebration," Odetta said, "because when you take sorrow and turn it into music, you transform it."

Singing persists. A generation after the advent of the Walk-man, over 20 million Americans (10.4 percent of us) *perform* in choral groups, according to the National Endowment for the Arts. That means a whole lot more of us are singing in the shower. Yet much everyday singing has been lost because of Thomas Edison's phonograph, that great and terrible invention. With it we have captured the voices of great folk singers like Odetta, accessible for all time. The listener doesn't have to be within hearing range of the singer. The singer doesn't even have to be alive. Yet these days fewer people know all the verses to "He's Got the Whole World in His Hands"—or any of the songs we used to sing to pass the time on journeys. In our sport utility vehicles, we turn on the radio or CD player—or even the TV and VCR—to quiet the kids.

We take ginkgo to sharpen our memories. We could be mem-orizing song lyrics instead. Driving a car full of napping passen-gers, waiting for the bus, up to your elbows in hot soapy water, pulling up the two hundredth stubborn weed of the morning—you could be learning that the third verse of "Amazing Grace" begins "Through many dangers, toils and snares I have already come." You could have decided which compliment in Cole Porter's "You're the Top" most applies to you. Would you rather be the Louvre Museum, Mickey Mouse, cellophane, Jimmy Durante's nose? All eight verses could be yours.

∾

"Non so *più cosa son, cosa faccio,*" the words to Cherubino's aria from Mozart's *The Marriage of Figaro* came back so quickly, though I was thirty-six now rather than sixteen. The muscles remember best what we learn young. "One in a foreign language, one in English," she had said. Could I possibly use "Out of My Dreams" from *Oklahoma*? I felt feminine, gay, when I sang it. It lay well for my voice. Two weeks. Go for it.

"Joan Goldsmith. You're next."

One last swallow of water. Breathe, exhale. Head up. Walk in. No, by God: Enter! Hand music to accompanist, résumé to conductor.

"And what will you be singing today?" the conductor smiled reassuringly.

"First, I wanted to let you know I've just begun studying voice again—after eight years away from music." Stating fact, not expecting special dispensation.

I nodded to the accompanist, breathed from low in the belly and gave the music everything I had to give at that moment in my life.

∾

THE LETTER arrived a week later: "We are pleased to offer you the position of volunteer singer. A rehearsal schedule is enclosed." I had no job, and a cold rented room instead of a home, but I had rehearsal Monday nights. And eight or nine times a year I would perform with the Minnesota Orchestra or the Saint Paul Chamber Orchestra. During performance weeks, we would rehearse Sunday, Monday, Tuesday, and Wednesday and sing concerts Wednesday, Friday, and Saturday. I would perform the great works—the requiems, the choral symphonies (Beethoven's Ninth, Mahler's Second), a little Bach, *Messiah,* of course—contemporary works, and an occasional pops concert.

∾

SOMEDAY, somewhere, it happens to each of us—the crucible time, when we lose everything we thought made us who we were, when what used to work so well no longer works at all. We are melted down and melted down and melted yet again, until nothing survives but core element, the miracle of essential self. Strange that my crucible had felt so cold.

∽

REHEARSALS took place in the choral room of "St. Kate's"—officially the College of St. Catherine—in St. Paul. I followed the map that accompanied my acceptance letter over green carpets of lawns, past slightly Gothic architecture. Found the right entrance to the right building. Smiled tightly at the strangers in line with me to receive music. Found my name on the seating chart posted on the door. Counted chairs, sat down, and listened.

Buzz, buzz, trill, rustle. A hundred unfamiliar voices greeting each other and laughing. Music being pulled out, coats arranged on the backs of chairs.

I looked down at the score. *Messiah*. The orange and white cover didn't even bother to name the composer—so singular is this among oratorios. Black letters stamped next to the title proclaimed, "No. 49. Property of the Saint Paul Chamber Orchestra." But score 49 was in my hands now. The tape at the spine was yellowed and cracked. Have to replace that. The paper had been worn velvet smooth over the years. My fingertips stroked lines and dots. How had I managed to survive a classical music education without singing this piece before? Lots of notes. Lots of little notes making patterns I had no comprehension of yet. Good. A problem with shape and outline. Capable of mastery.

My body fell into place, holding the solid weight of an open score, forearms raised, hands open—not in supplication, but certainly in a gesture of giving.

"All right. Music down. Everybody stand for warmups." Conductor Joel Revzen entered. Shock of dark hair, flashing smile.

"Back rubs to the right." The line turned right and the stranger behind me started massaging my shoulders. Goodness.

"Reverse." Another pair of hands. The blessing of touch. God, how I'd missed it.

"D major please," he gestured to the accompanist.

The sound swirled around and through me—warm, rich, enormous: one hundred focused voices embraced and amplified by a resonant space. One hundred voices, including mine.

∾

AT ELEVEN o'clock one December morning, my soon-to-be former spouse stood in court, uncontested, to finalize our divorce, while I stood on stage at Orchestra Hall, singing backup for Mitch Miller and all the good people who had come to sing along.

The hall seemed painted in splotches of gray and white—old ladies and a sprinkling of old gentlemen, many of whom had been bussed in for the occasion. Permanent waves were clearly visible: The houselights were up so they could see their song sheets.

They had come to sing with us: healthy and frail; married and long widowed; expecting a joyful holiday with grandchildren, expecting a harsh Christmas, alone.

"Joy to the world," we proclaimed together from stage and audience.

The second cellist looked bored. Mitch radiated enthusiasm. Singers' bodies and voices surrounded me. The stage lights shone down.

My blowfish, my clarinet, and I—we took a deep breath and sang.

Harmonium
and Tessitura

*I*magine a sunset somewhere in the wide open spaces—the ocean, the Southwest—where the sunsets are long and lovely, unimpeded by buildings or city lights. The colors change slowly, slowly, almost imperceptibly. Yet if you close your eyes for a moment, you open them to a completely new panorama, startlingly different, delightful, serene.

Now imagine this sunset through the eyes and brush of an Impressionist painter. You are the color yellow, appearing here, there, a streak, a spot; pure bright yellow at first, then tinged with red; blending, clashing with the other colors; shining brightly then fading away.

That is what it is like to sing John Adams's *Harmonium*.

Now imagine an automated factory of steel and gray and noise. You are a highly sophisticated robot. Your task is to hammer one piece of metal to another. Your programming is complex;

your rhythms tedious, repetitive, until abruptly you must shift—
half a beat here, a whole beat there. Instead of four blows of your
hammer on each object, now it's three, five, seven. All the while
other robots beat on the same object, their rhythms rarely syn-
chronizing with yours. Your programming orders you: Clang
fiercely, ping delicately, and always, always respond precisely to
master control.

That, also, is what it is like to sing John Adams's *Harmonium*.
And that is why my poor, overworked vocal cords gave up
the ghost.

It was spring, 1991. The Minnesota Chorale had been engaged
to sing *Harmonium* with the Minnesota Orchestra under Edo de
Waart. I was singing soprano—until suddenly, frighteningly I was
no longer singing.

I have lost my voice before; indeed, I had suffered three upper
respiratory infections in that same, difficult year. But *Harmonium*
was a catalyst. This time, in losing my voice I found it—in my life,
my works, my loves and friends. The key was tessitura.

First performed in 1981, *Harmonium* is composer John Adams's
choral setting of three poems. It begins with John Donne's poem
"Negative Love":

> *If that be simply perfectest*
> *Which can by no way be expressed*
> *But* Negatives, *my love is so.*
> *To All, which all love, I say no.*

Then the piece moves through Emily Dickinson's refined
encounter with immortality in "Because I Could Not Stop for
Death" ("He kindly stopped for me") to the extravagant physical
passion of her "Wild Nights":

Were I with thee
Wild Nights should be
Our luxury!

Emerging from Adams's early explorations of minimalism, the music is beautiful and exciting to listen to; tedious, demanding, and exhausting to sing—the only piece I have ever performed that made me wish I were sitting in the audience instead of on stage. The rhythms are often fast and complex, the beat proclaiming itself as obviously as in rock 'n' roll. The harmonies change excruciatingly slowly, often layering on top of one another: While the alto section is singing a perfectly normal major chord, the soprano section comes in with another perfectly normal major chord, only one step up. The dissonance is rich, with layers of sound complementing and clashing against each other like the flavors of a fine old Bordeaux. Fascinating to listen to. Theoretically easy to sing. After all, most of the time you're moving just a step, a major second, up or down. Anybody can sing "do, re, mi." But when they're singing "do" and holding it, and you're singing "re" and holding it, and someone else comes in with "mi" and holds it . . . it's awfully hard to *actually* hold it and not drift one way or the other.

The feeling you get resisting this pitch drift is the same feeling you may have had in kindergarten when the only way you could possibly hang onto your part in "Row, row, row your boat," when the second group came in, was to stick your fingers in your ears—a gesture that is frowned upon in classical music circles.

So there was the stress of simply hanging on to the right note. Then there was coping with the endless repetition and the dynamic contrasts. The piece opens with the words "No, no, no" sung over and over at least a hundred times, sung by the second sopranos in what was then the weakest note in my range—the middle-range A, the note where chest voice *must* switch to head voice. (You may have experienced that "break" when you were on a high school bus, coming back from a football game, singing at the top of your lungs. There's a point where, if you wanted to sing a higher pitch, the big Ethel Merman "belting" sound gave way to a smaller sweeter sound. That's your "break." Chest voice gives way to head voice. It happens on a particular pitch for each person.)

Adams begins the "Negative Love" section with endless repetitions of the word "no," creating that factory hammer pinging over and over, softly then louder then back again, but always, always repeating that A. "Wild Nights" is loud and ferocious, with the sopranos screaming up to a high B-flat, and then ending ever so gently with a whispered "Ah, the sea." Singing your loudest and then your softest, your highest and then your lowest, in the space of a few minutes, is difficult for even the healthiest voice, which mine wasn't.

I had recovered from a bout of laryngitis the week before, but evidently not completely. During the first performance some notes simply disappeared. I opened my mouth, engaged the thoughts and muscles that are used to sing, and nothing happened—a kind of vocal aphasia, as terrifying as the stroke victim's loss of the word "cat." High, soft pianissimos were impossible. Long, held notes faded into breathy exhalations long before the music called for them to end.

There were one hundred twenty-five long black dresses and tuxedos in five neat rows on the stage of Orchestra Hall that first night. I stood in the third row, four in from the right, helplessly struggling for notes like a bird with a broken wing struggling to fly. The competent one stood beside me—the soprano whose committee work is efficient, whose hair is never out of place, whose clothes match and complement each other, who always seems to know what she's doing, who expresses her concern for you if you're not singing up to par in rehearsal. She gave me a funny look, leaned over and sang the right note in my ear, loud. *Oh, God, not only am I screwing up, but I'm letting everyone down, and they're noticing.* "Are you all right?" she asked later as we walked offstage. "Maybe you should have yourself checked by a doctor. It sounds like nodes to me." Terrifying word— "nodes"—calluses on the vocal cords that have interrupted or ended many singing careers, always requiring rest, sometimes requiring surgery. I lashed out, "Leave me alone, just leave me alone." I went home that night and cried for hours, blocking my sinuses, tightening my throat—thoroughly sabotaging my ability to sing for at least twenty-four hours.

The next morning I called in sick. I missed that night's performance, but gathered my courage and returned to sing the third and final night. Only two-thirds of the notes came out of my mouth. The rest was air. Impossible to hide from the truth. I couldn't sing this piece. I couldn't sing at all.

A week later, I was sitting in the otolaryngologist's office among people with tracheotomy holes in their throats. There was nothing to read in the hour and fifteen minutes I waited except pamphlets from the receptionist's desk on how to survive throat cancer. I read them. I would not be able to pass a quiz on the subject. I had done little but sleep for the last five days. All my notes seemed to have returned, but my throat felt tight and would get sore if I talked for more than a minute or two.

A family physician looks at your throat. An ear, nose, and

throat specialist, on the other hand, looks at your vocal cords. The specialist sprays your throat with a foul-tasting contact anesthetic (cocaine, actually), holds your tongue out of the way with a piece of gauze and slips a warmed mirror down into your throat. (Singers don't gag. We've trained our throats to stay open on command.)

The verdict was delivered. No damage to the vocal cords. No need for surgery or months of rest and therapy. Just an upper respiratory bug that had hit me hard but was now on its way out. That's all. *Just* . . . So rest, drink plenty of fluids: the old song.

I consulted my voice teacher, who had one further recommendation: Start singing alto. I'm a mezzo-soprano: My voice is not as high as a soprano's and not as low as an alto's. Mezzo-sopranos and baritones have a tricky choice when they sing in a chorus. We're the monkeys in the middle. If the composer has distributed the parts in the typical soprano, alto, tenor, bass, we middle children often have to sing either a little too high or a little too low for comfort. Either can tire the voice. I had been singing soprano, but it seemed the time had come to err in the other direction—on the side of singing a little too low—hoping to avoid vocal exhaustion.

A month later, we began rehearsals for the Mozart *Requiem*. I moved ten seats in, to the left. Alto territory, just to the right of center. When people remarked on the change, I had my line ready: "Yes, I've switched from soprano to alto. I've also moved from St. Paul to Minneapolis. I can't think of any more fundamental changes short of a sex-change operation." It usually got a laugh, which I needed. I was nervous. I hadn't sung alto in twenty years. Could I still read music well enough? Sopranos rely on their ears so much. There it is, the melody, high above everything else, easy to hear, easy to grab hold of. But the alto, the harmony, the note woven into the thick fabric of the chord . . . I coached myself silently: *Pick out your strand and only your strand. Don't think low—you'll sing flat or tenor. Think core, the center; focus the sound. And above all, connect your eyes to your brain and throat. Sing what's written, not the assumptions your ears like to make.*

By the second rehearsal I realized I was home. My voice felt fine, comfortable, full of ease, free of strain. There was a sense of recognition, of rightness, of my voice telling me, *Well, of course, this is what I'm meant to sing.* As a soprano I knew I could sing well if everything went right—if I had had enough sleep, if I were properly warmed up. As an alto I was just singing well. A joyful confidence crept into the sound, surprising me sometimes with its warmth and richness. I discovered rich, low notes that never got used before. Even the passages that I knew would takes weeks to master didn't overwhelm me. With time and practice, they would be mine. I had found my tessitura.

When singers talk about "tessitura" (pronounced tess-ih-TOO-rah), what we really mean is a sense of home. We'll say "Sure I have a high C, but I don't want to live up there." Tessitura is where you want to live. "Range" is a completely different idea. When you want to know the range of a song, you look for the highest note and the lowest note. When you want to know a song's tessitura, you look at where most of the notes are. Range is important. If you don't have those high and low notes in your voice, you can't sing that song in that key. But tessitura is even more important. Singing a song that lies primarily in the middle of the staff and then climaxes on a high G is definitely not the same thing as singing one that perpetually sits at the top of the staff—F, G, A, F, G, A. I can do the first with ease. Just thinking about the second makes me tired.

Where do I belong? Does this feel like home? This song, this job, this church, this neighborhood, this man?

In John Adams's *Harmonium,* the soprano tessitura put me on the weakest note in my middle range for most of one full movement and then up in the stratosphere for another. I failed because the tessitura was all wrong. Not me, the tessitura. When I understood that, I understood a lot.

My twenties and early thirties were about range. My answer to the question "Can you do this?" was always "Yes." I taught singing; I acted in commercials; I sold cars; I worked as a legal secretary, a sales rep, a sales manager, a product manager. I achieved a lot and got fired a lot. As if the music of my life required me to push the high notes until they squeaked, the low notes until they growled. Then the catastrophe—out of a home, a job, and a marriage all at the same time. Fired as profoundly as it's possible to be. As a wife, I had been part of "we" for so long that I had to consciously train myself to use the pronoun "I." Talk about losing your voice.

As I began to create a new life, I found I had become a lot more self-protective, more interested in tessitura. The question was no longer "Can I do it?" but "Does the choice have a sense of rightness, of flow, of slipping into a life that is already a part of me, like a pair of ancient and beloved blue jeans?"

I am what I am. No more, but certainly no less. I'm short, with brown hair and brown eyes that can smile; twenty-five pounds more than thin; with catlike energy (I sprint and then I nap); emotional; with a talent for writing and singing and a love of dancing. When I'm frightened I get nasty. I leave my shoes everywhere.

It helped to think about the instruments of the orchestra. A clarinet is not a trumpet. They can play many of the same notes, and a fanfare played on the clarinet could be interesting, but a trumpet fanfare is more typical, and there's a reason for that.

Even the right tessitura (in life or music) isn't comfortable all the time. But there are fewer of the stomach cramps and headaches, the terror and frustrations of being the wrong person doing the wrong things in the wrong place and time.

Sometimes, to learn and grow I must work outside my tessitura. I've found that when I do, I must work both harder and gentler, more persistently and with greater self-compassion. After all, classical music is hard. It's a skill sport. So is life. You can't just grit your teeth and force it. So I work on the coloratura (the long phrases of quickly moving notes)—articulating, phrasing, supporting, listening—but when the number of imperfect repetitions overwhelms me with failure, I stop, do something else for a while, and then come back.

But I have to come back. I've learned that singing is part of my life's tessitura. If I ignore it, a certain spiritual crankiness sets in, like the restlessness my body feels if I neglect to exercise it.

Every year, we re-audition for the Minnesota Chorale. Most of us are invited to return for the next season. Some are not. Every year I walk into the little room (empty except for the piano, the accompanist, and the conductors taking notes) knowing that they will hear at least fifty voices that are better than mine. I walk in knowing that. But I also know that I can tell a story better than most. So I take the auditioners on a journey that happens to be a song. It's an act of faith—that if I focus on what I *can* do, the rest will be all right.

So much of what we perceive as failure is really just being in the wrong tessitura, struggling for the notes we "ought" to be able to sing, or stubbornly holding on to a way of life that no longer fits. This is what I learned singing John Adams's *Harmonium*.

"Too Important
to Leave to
the Professionals"

*I*t hurt to go to the theater for a while, when I first gave up on myself as a professional performer. I would sit in the audience, listening and watching, thinking, *I could do that. I could do* that, *too.* Knowing that I wasn't going to.

I had decided at twelve I was going to be a singer/actress. My friends went through identity crises in college. Not me. I sailed confidently into my twenties and my career in show biz. The record isn't too dismal: a modest success voicing commercials, a couple of bit parts in professional theater (the second maid in *Life With Father*, the sixth singing dwarf in the appalling *Snow White Goes West*). Auditioning became the job; paying work the perk. I taught singing to support my performing habit. I hung in longer than some—six whole years—even braved New York City for a year—till the sporadic morsels of applause no longer compensated for the daily discipline and discouragement. I dropped out.

But I wasn't going to be an amateur. Not me. I'd grown up listening to my mother complain about amateurs. She made part of her living directing community theater. She'd complain that this actor was a pain: he came late, scared everyone by refusing to learn his lines till dress rehearsal. That one had an ego as big as all outdoors, but she was the only one who auditioned who could play the part, so Mom was going to have to pat and soothe that ego three nights a week for the next two months. If only they could be fired: amateurs!

I wasn't going to join that company. I stopped making music altogether.

∽

WHEN I was seven or so, my younger sister, Vicki, bet me a quarter that I couldn't go for a day without singing. A whole day: a whole quarter. That was two Superman comic books in 1958. Sometime around three o'clock I forgot the bet and burst into "Thumbelina, Thumbelina, tiny little thing." So I lost. But I was the lucky one. When my older sister, Diane, was six, her first-grade teacher had asked her not to sing, too. Not as part of a wager, but because, the teacher told her, she was making it harder for the group. Diane rarely sang in public after that.

By the time we're grown up, we've self-diagnosed: I'm a singer, or I can't carry a tune in a bucket. I can dance, or I'm only fit for stepping on my partner's feet. We do what we expect to do well. To avoid embarrassing ourselves we avoid the rest. So when our bodies are filled with more joy or sorrow than they can contain, we have nothing to mop up the overflow with. We end up pouring it into the ear of a therapist.

We separate ourselves into watchers and doers.

Amateurs are doers. Once upon a time they were wealthy, male, excellent doers: the gentleman athlete, the gentleman archaeologist. When did the word get to be a synonym for "incompetent dilettante"? Unpaid singers make up most of the choruses in the United States, even when the chorus as a whole is paid by a symphony orchestra. Yet choral associations call us "volunteers" to avoid the dreaded stigma of the word "amateur."

Conductor Robert Shaw fought this connotation every time he repeated his maxim, "Music and sex are too important to leave to the professionals."

Indeed, we Americans seem to have forgotten that "amateur" comes from the Latin for "lover," not "can't make a living at it."

∽

AT SOME point in her or his life, the amateur falls in love—not slowly, not gradually, but with that resounding whoosh that marks passion.

Steve had a few fellow players from the high school orchestra over to his house that afternoon. As he sauntered over to the record player, he told us about listening to Brahms's First Symphony as a preschooler. Loving it best of anything, he had played it over and over until he wore the record out.

I didn't believe him. It was the sort of thing he would say, Steve, the trumpet, and also his buddy, Howard, the French horn. They played classical music records in the high school band room at lunch. Sometimes I'd stay and listen. And sometimes I'd say, "Wow, that was really neat. What was it?"

They'd wither me with pitying glances and respond, "Why, it's the such-and-such movement of so-and-so's concerto in E-flat, of course."

So I didn't believe Steve's little boy/big Brahms symphony story. I do now—ever since I met a five-year-old who listened to the opera *The Magic Flute* on a car trip and proceeded to drive her parents mad from then on insisting that they play the Queen of the Night's aria over and over. She likes the high sparkly part and her sung version of it is not much worse than mine.

But back to falling in love. The haze of memory puts fourteen-year-old me, Lisa (flutist, alto, and best friend), Howard (the chubby, pale horn player), and Steve (who later went to Eastman and converted from trumpet to piano) in Steve's living room. Since I didn't much like the boys (or they me, I imagine), I have no inkling as to how this social event happened. What is crystal clear is how the last movement of Brahms's First Symphony hit me.

It was like watching from a porch on a hot, dusty night—you are safe, but something's building, something dangerous and wonderful. You can feel it in the sudden drop to coolness, the surprising, moist air touching your cheek. The first few themes: anguish in the strings, anger in the timpani; the trumpet call of hope; the stately hymn played by brass choir—wonderful in and of themselves, but hungry, reaching. The air crackles with the potential of lightning. Then finally, the storm breaks, soaking rain into thirsty earth: and the strings proclaim their major, majestic statement of *YES*.

YES permeated my skin, opened my breath, hitched a ride on my circulatory system to tingle fingertips and toes—an invasion of affirmation.

Who knows why love hits when love hits? My mother played Beethoven symphonies while she cleaned—Toscanini and the NBC Symphony Orchestra. To this day, when I embark on a major housewifely initiative like washing windows, a Beethoven symphony is as essential as paper towels. Mom adored Joan Sutherland, and the sound of coloratura arias filled the house. Both parents watched Leonard Bernstein on TV. I never stayed for long. All those men in formal suits. Boring. But from the moment that final theme of Brahms's First triumphed into my body, *happily ever after* became possible. Real as the vibrations against my ears. I was captured.

Still am. Years of music school later I could analyze the various components, point out to you his modulations. But craftsmanship cannot explain enthrallment. The other day, driving to an appointment, I flipped on the radio. A second of silence, then the last movement of Brahms's First. So, a choice: (1) possibly cause an accident, because body, mind, and soul were otherwise occupied; (2) turn off the radio; or (3) pull over, listen, and perhaps arrive late.

Lovers are notoriously impractical.

∞

BEFORE BRAHMS taught me to love the sound of classical music, I had felt the power of performing it. At arts camp, majoring in drama and string bass, I sang a bit, too, in chorus and madrigals. It never occurred to me to major in voice. You weren't supposed to take singing lessons till you were sixteen.

Parents' weekend was fast approaching, with its annual feature, a choral performance in which everyone—singer, dancer, actor, artist, instrumentalist—was required to sing unless they played in the orchestra. The rolling, green acres in the Berkshire Hills of Massachusetts hummed with Haydn's oratorio, *The Creation*, with its famous hit tune "The Heavens Are Telling." But there was a glitch: We had, among the campers, a luscious soprano to greet the spring "With verdure clad" but no tenor to declaim the first sunrise. The madrigal teacher approached me. Would I be willing to audition for the tenor part, singing it in the octave written (an octave higher than it would normally sound)?

Oh, boy. Got the part. Didn't tell my parents. Big secret.

I stood with the other soloists—soprano and bass—at the front of the stage, seeing then not seeing the audience as Haydn's sun rose behind me—from the softest of pale pinks in the strings to the triumph of radiant gold shining from the full orchestra. Then silence, just my voice as the angel Uriel, proclaiming the dawn of the fourth day of creation.

Singing pouring out of me, an orchestra and chorus supporting me, parental applause—ah, this was life. This was going to be *my* life.

But applause has the wispy nourishment of cotton candy. The star of the high school musical grows up and out into the world, and she learns a lot about rejection.

When the applause becomes unreliable, you find out what you truly love.

∾

AMATEUR. LOVER. A person who gives because it is a joy in the body to give. Sensuous: the way a full breath expands lungs and rib cage, bringing relief to a body calcified from sitting at a computer keyboard. The way singing massages the sinus cavities and chest with vibrating resonance.

The puny little breaths we take in real life, the meager sounds of our amplified voices making business presentations—compare these to the joy of reaching down into the tips of your toes, further even—into the core of the Earth, for a sound that is yours and not yours, for a sound that takes technique and control and freedom and asking, and, above all, letting go. Such extravagant joy.

And the pleasure of seeing the conductor's face, of responding with a wave of united energy. When he makes his movements smaller for a pianissimo and we don't get soft enough, so the gestures become tinier yet, until he gathers into those hands the power of two hundred voices precisely making almost no sound at all. With consciousness of the impending crescendo, but no increase in volume. Not yet . . . not yet . . . Now . . . *YES!* This is payment enough.

∞

WE AMATEURS are paid in other ways as well. Liz and I put on living room recitals. We seem to be able to manage one extravaganza every year and a half. We choose the music. We scavenge our closets for costumes (Judy Garland and Mickey Rooney, move over). A red cape, a feather boa, a cream silk shawl, fuzzy ears suggest a world of characters. We regale the forty or so of our friends we've managed to cram into her living room with an hour of songs, arias, comedy routines, and readings. Then we all drink champagne and eat goodies. The champagne may be cheap but the event isn't, because we hire an excellent accompanist and pay her for several rehearsals. But oh, the luxury of preparing and performing the material we love best, unconcerned about whether it is useful for our careers, whether anyone would ever hire us to sing it.

Over fifty now, with toddling grandchildren, Liz becomes Don Giovanni's teenage flirt, Zerlina. Though my voice would be lost at the Met, I fill the living room with Menotti's ghost story of an aria, "The Black Swan." I sing to a pregnant bride searching for her disappeared lover, telling her he's "deep, deep down in the river's bed," "eyes wide open, never asleep." I wail the high G and walk away knowing I've given the song the best I have to give at this point in my life and my skill.

The privilege of doing one's absolute best is rare in real life. In the business world we mostly do what we can get done with this quarter's budget that's innovative but not so creative that it scares the boss, or, worse yet, the boss's boss. In the professional music world, unions and budgets guarantee that there is never enough time. A symphonic chorus will rehearse once, maybe twice, with orchestra before mounting a major work. It's nobody's fault. This week the orchestra is playing Bach, next week Aaron Kernis. They have to move on, and they have to rest sometimes. But you can hear the difference when you listen to chamber music. The sound of a string quartet playing in sensitive ensemble is the sound of those who have rehearsed on their own time, without a union clocking ticking away—something amateurs do all the time.

∾

HOW PECULIAR are we—those of us who spend time rehearsing instead of sitting at home listening to perfect recordings? Picking up the telephone, I discover that pinning down the number of volunteer singers is only slightly easier than trying to track down the number of volunteer tomato plants. In both cases, one must proceed by inference.

In 1982, 1985, 1992, and 1997, the National Endowment for the Arts sponsored a Survey of Public Participation in the Arts, known by the stuttering acronym of SPPA. In 1997, the SPPA interviewed a cross section of 12,349 American adults and extrapolated that data.

Walt Whitman didn't have to strain his ears to hear America singing.

According to SPPA, over 20 million Americans (10.4 percent of us) sang in public choral performances in 1997—with church choirs, symphonic choirs, community choruses, and myriads of other ensembles. The figure includes paid and unpaid, professional and amateur. Three and a half million Americans sing operatic arias in their living rooms or showers, but only 600,000 perform them in public. Another 15.1 million of us belt out Broadway show tunes from the comforts of home; but a mere 3.3 million in public. The survey didn't inquire into our country-western singing habits, or folk, pop, or rock, which seems odd, since they did ask about needlework. (If you sing while you quilt, you are definitely in thriving company. SPPA found 54 million Americans engaged in weaving, crocheting, quilting, needlepoint, or sewing.)

Okay, so 20 million of us ruthlessly abandon spouses, children, jobs, and other worldly concerns to perform in vocal congregation. Who are we? What are we singing?

Sacred music pours from the throats of 2.7 million of us every Sunday, according to *The Chronicle of Philanthropy*'s April 17, 1997, issue on volunteerism.

As for secular choirs (like mine), as of 1999, the association

Chorus America numbered 118 "professional" members, choruses that pay at least 25 percent or 12 of their singers. (I can't think of another type of organization that would call itself professional when it pays only a quarter of the participants.) Chorus America's membership includes another 436 organizations composed entirely of "volunteers," many of whom pay dues, as well as buy their own music and costumes.

But Chorus America's membership of 554 "independent choral organizations" excludes academic and church choirs, so it represents a very small proportion of American choirs. The American Choral Directors Association numbers 13,500 choral directors, most of whom conduct several choirs—in schools, colleges, houses of worship, wherever their ensembles can find rehearsal space.

GALA Choruses, the Gay and Lesbian Association of Choruses, includes 180 choruses and 10,000 singer members who sing everything from Broadway to Bach. The Society for the Preservation and Encouragement of Barbershop Quartet Singing in America (SPEBSQSA) numbers 1,800 quartets and 34,000 male singers in the United States and Canada. Their female counterpart, Sweet Adelines International, has 30,000 members in the United States, Canada, and abroad. Both organizations' offices are only too happy to send heaps of information at the drop of a fax number, including a newsletter featuring a technical article on the judicious use of vibrato in solos, as opposed to quartet and choral singing.

Another highly organized group are those who love to sing in Welsh. All over the United States, devotees gather in homes and church basements to sing lovely hymns with tongue-twisting lyrics. Their annual gathering—the Welsh National Gymanfu

Ganu (pronounced "ghi-MAHN-va GHAH-nee")—typically draws 1,200 to 2,000 singers.

And so on and so on, to the teenagers singing rock in the basement and their parents jamming folk tunes in the living room.

∽

BUT IS ALL this singing merely some glorious, self-indulgent hobby? Do amateurs—even the ones who never perform outside the living room—make a contribution?

The classical music world could not survive without amateurs. First, because doers make the best audiences. It's true of anything. I can watch a basketball game and get an adrenaline rush from the competition, but my friend Michael can feel the ball in his hands.

Watch singers watching a singer. If the performer is good, no audience will be with her more. Take Barbara Bonney singing Schubert's great torch song, *"Gretchen am Spinnrade."* Gretchen is sitting at her spinning wheel going slowly mad remembering the lover who abandoned her. The driving energy of the wheel throbs in the piano accompaniment. Nearly every female studying voice sings Gretchen at some point. In an audience full of singers, teachers, accompanists, and spouses, Bonney made it a new song. When she sang "And oh, his kiss," instead of belting out the high note of *küss* she hovered, infinitely soft, and the audience melted, not because it was hard to do—although we all knew that it was—but because it was so completely right for a young girl's memory of tenderness and love and lust all swirling around in her being.

Second, the classical music world needs amateurs because it is not, never has been, and probably never will be self-supporting. If you're going to have a vibrant culture, you need rich patrons (formerly known as the aristocracy) and government support (formerly known as royalty), and a whole lot of people working for free. As royalty punishes the arts for a few artists whose work they find offensive, the contribution of volunteers becomes more important than ever. Though not necessarily more respected. In America we have this funny notion that something is worth what the market says it's worth. And if a product can't make a profit you should euthanize it. This works rather nicely in the realm of breakfast cereals.

We may not respect amateurs, but we rely on them. What else is a jury of one's peers? Since the signing of the Magna Carta in 1215, systems of jurisprudence—first the English and later the American—have expected amateurs to distinguish between injustice and justice. The fate of the accused rests in the hands of a bunch of people who may never have seen a real courtroom before they were chosen for this jury.

The Olympic Games, of course, have struggled with issues of amateur versus professional since 1896, when Baron Pierre de Coubertin, disturbed by creeping commercialism in international sports, established the modern Olympics. Jim Thorpe was stripped of the decathlon and pentathlon medals he won in 1912 for having played minor-league baseball (at $2 a game), but by 1992, we had basketball's "dream team"—fabulous players, but hardly amateurs, by any definition.

"Michael Jordan, the marquee player for the Dream Team, had warned officials months ago that using college players would be less complicated," wrote William C. Rhoden in the *New York Times*, August 9, 1992. Jordan told them, quite rightly, that professional players had contractual obligations to their individual sponsors that would directly compete with Olympic sponsorship deals. "Indeed, the basketball team's closest match of the entire tournament was with the U.S. Olympic Committee over commercial endorsements." Such is the price we paid to see the best players in the world.

But are the best players always professionals?

Tom Bopp discovered Comet Hale-Bopp while looking through a friend's telescope. He didn't own one himself. He went to star parties, nocturnal gatherings under dark skies.

Bernie Sanden, another amateur at that life-changing star party, wrote in the Hale-Bopp Web site, "Am I envious that my name is not on it? Not at all! I never expected to make a mark discovering comets. I merely walked over and observed something Thomas Bopp had called to our attention. At the time I didn't know I was one of the fortunate few to see a new comet; maybe the fifth person on the planet to see it in 3,000 years. We gaze up at the wonders and see them come and go. Are we not wonders of creation ourselves? For that I am thankful." The lesson for Sanden "is simple—keep looking up and things will be revealed to you!"

The lesson for me is that the true amateur is more interested in seeing stars than becoming one.

∾

SATURDAY morning, I woke up tired with everything aching. Uh-oh. Bad day for this. Our only rehearsal with Doc Severinsen and The Minnesota Orchestra for a concert of show tunes tonight. Ran to catch the bus, stocked up on cough drops. Dashed on stage: two hours and ten minutes to rehearse one hour and forty minutes of music.

Dapper and trim in untucked T-shirt and jeans, sometimes Doc cues us, sometimes not. "You're going to have to get that entrance on your own, kiddos, I'm busy." And he is. With a music stand between him and audience (holding his solo music) and another music stand between him and the orchestra (holding his conductor's score), his choreography goes like this: Turn page of orchestra music, turn page of solo music, turn back to orchestra and conduct. Solo coming up (wrinkled brow, slightly shaky hands). Put down baton, take off reading glasses, place glasses carefully on conductor's podium, pick up either trumpet or flugel- horn, blow through horn to warm it up, clear spit valve if neces- sary. Exhale, inhale, grin with clear brow, turn like peacock unfurling tail toward audience, play solo. Soar, glide, shine, swing, croon, caress. Turn back to orchestra, wrinkle brow, replace trumpet, replace reading glasses, pick up stick, resume conducting.

In rehearsal Doc turns to us to play "I've Grown Accustomed to Her Face," not to point up any cues we'll have to remember in performance, but to play one tune just for us. The first three notes "I've . . . grown . . . a . . ." splash out: low, fat, hesitant, won- dering. Doc's sound embodies the quiet astonishment Henry Higgins felt in *My Fair Lady* when he discovered he had come to feel something for a transformed guttersnipe. The orchestra musi- cians listen, their bodies attentive. They respect him, these classi- cal players.

Three hours' break, then performance. Doc dons black and glitter for the first half, red leather trousers topped by gold and red silk for the second. By the time of our final, rousing "There's No Business Like Show Business" a spasm next to my right shoulder blade burns from hours of holding music in upturned arms, but the rest of the aches have disappeared, lost sometime during the first minutes of rehearsal.

Of course, you can forget anything if you concentrate hard enough on something else, and I've been focusing all the resonance at my command trying to cut through the volume of symphony orchestra and jazz combo. But what about the energy infusing me? As if the music has been loving me back.

I have the best seat in the house. Maybe not for hearing—the balance leans heavily toward altos, tenors, and the French horns seated in front of us—but for being within the glory. As an amateur, I am indeed a lover. But I am more blessed than that. I am also the beloved.

Followership

*T*he air in Aspen, Colorado, is thick with notes and the making of notes. You can reach out your hand and catch them, like fireflies: Students on the town bus studying scores, their instrument cases at their feet. Singers "doo, doo"-ing under their breaths as they walk down the street, unaware of their rehearsing. Not everyone and not everywhere—in the restaurants are thin, blond, tanned aristocrats, wearing tattered hiking shorts and Patek Phillipe watches—but many people and almost everywhere.

Since 1949, the Aspen Music Festival has entertained patrons of this expensive ski resort during the off-season, when Aspen Mountain is covered with pasture, edelweiss, and bluebells instead of snow.

The Minnesota Chorale had been engaged to sing the Mozart *Requiem* as the grand finale of that summer's Aspen Music Festival. For seven precious days, we would have the pleasure of immersing ourselves in music. No garbage to take out, no paycheck to earn—just music.

For one week real life would be suspended. I would have the freedom to work, to dream, to get acquainted with the singers I rehearse with all year, to ask of myself and the universe the important, impertinent questions I have always wanted to ask.

Aspen gives permission for that. Perhaps because the oxygen molecules in the air are spread so far apart, there is room for the spirit to expand.

To sing the Mozart *Requiem* in such a place! Fauré, Verdi, Brahms, even Andrew Lloyd Webber—so many composers have made their statement through this form. But Mozart is special. Mention the Mozart *Requiem* in a group of music lovers and you will hear "I will never forget the performance I heard three days after John Kennedy was assassinated . . ." or "Our chorus sang it right after my husband died . . ." We take the Mozart *Requiem* personally.

Our chorus had prepared the *Requiem* with great pleasure as we rehearsed with our chorus conductor in Minnesota. We were eager to begin working with the festival orchestra conductor in Aspen.

A symphonic chorus will typically work with two conductors: the chorus conductor and the orchestra conductor. After the performance of a choral work with symphony orchestra, you will frequently see a stranger walk on stage, gesture at the chorus, then take a bow. This chorus conductor has done hours of preparatory work before handing the singers off to the orchestra conductor. Our staff chorus conductor leads three to twelve piano rehearsals (depending on the difficulty of the music), achieving not just mastery of the notes but also a thorough understanding of musical nuance.

The orchestra conductor typically conducts one chorus-and-piano dress rehearsal as well as the two chorus-and-orchestra rehearsals that are all the budget will allow for refining interpretation and pulling the whole thing together. The two conductors are supposed to communicate, so that tempos and interpretation do not come as a surprise when the baton changes hands. Even so, the transition requires a mental agility that is the hallmark of good choral singers.

∾

THE MOUNTAINS flowed by our car windows as four of us chattered to pass the time from the Denver airport to Aspen. Sandra, who consults to corporate executives when she isn't singing alto, taught us the game of Organizational Blasphemy: You think of a value that might be important to the organization, then you state its most outrageous contradiction. If the response to your statement is gales of laughter or gasps of horror, you've hit the mark.

"For instance," said Sandra. "Let's take the Chorale." Her voice deepened, proclaiming, "The Minnesota Chorale is mostly a social organization. Fun comes first; music comes second."

"Oh, sure." That was Chris, another alto. "At least six of us go out for a beer after rehearsal."

"And we do have a party every single year," I chimed in. "Of course, I didn't go to the last two. Were they fun?"

"How about this," said Liz, representing the soprano section. "You don't have to practice. You can fake it. And if you can't, there's plenty of time to learn the music in rehearsal."

Rueful laughter all round. We do eight or more major works a year. *You* try singing Bach without practicing. All those little notes go by like the telephone poles seen from a speeding train.

So this chorus comes to rehearsal ready to make music. Is

every singer prepared and committed all the time? Of course not. But a chorus knows the answers to "Who are we? What do we stand for?" just like every healthy family, church, or company. Individuals may not know they know. They may pay scant attention to the high-minded sentiments issued by conductors, parents, or senior managers. But the values of a culture live in the mind, heart, nerves, and muscles of each person. Sometimes everything has to go wrong to make those values visible.

∽

THE BLASPHEMY game slipped into the trivia of memory as we left the car and entered a rehearsal hall that hummed with anticipation.

The conductor of the festival orchestra walked in—a chubby, balding guy of fifty-five or sixty, with a few wisps of hair and a genial but harried look. We applauded when introduced, as custom dictates. He said how pleased he was to work with us and told us that he hadn't conducted the *Requiem* in twenty years. *Fine,* we thought. He would be coming back to an old friend. But by the end of the rehearsal our good will had soured.

It was generic Mozart. No elegance. No wit or energy. We had rehearsed with crisp, elegant tempos that spoke. His ponderous, gooey tempos seemed to beat around every emotional bush. *"quam olim Abrahae promisisti . . ."* ("As you promised Abraham and his descendants") ceased to be the masses grabbing God by the shirt collar and holding Him accountable, and turned into afternoon tea with the deity. The fugues lost their clarity. The lilting *Hostias* lost its grace. And so dreadfully on.

He kept changing his mind during and between rehearsals. Faster, slower. Still, the music seemed coated with mud. "When did he look at the score? On the plane?" we muttered, frustrated. "What does the man *want?*" because if he didn't know, we couldn't give it to him.

For all I know, the conductor may have been dealing with major family crises. (Years later I heard him conduct Strauss and it was splendid.) But once a musician enters the rehearsal hall, the outside world becomes irrelevant. There may be reasons for poor performance, but the harsh truth is that there are no excuses.

We struggled through piano dress rehearsal, first rehearsal with orchestra, then Sunday morning's orchestra dress: eighty discouraged, grouchy singers. We knew what this piece could be. We had practiced our runs, rehearsed our ensemble. We were not happy about the goo we were wallowing in.

Language difficulties compounded our frustration. We had prepared the text in German Latin, pronouncing it as it would have been by Mozart's singers (pronouncing "requiem" as "reh-kvee-em," rather than the reh-kwee-em of church Latin, for example). The guest conductor *hated* German Latin (as a matter of fact, so do I). But it would have been nice to know ahead of time. Switching gears on that one was not appreciably easier than suddenly having to sing it in French.

Had the two conductors—chorus and orchestra—communicated at all before we began preparations back home? If not, they were both to blame. The chorus conductor's job is to pick up the phone and ask. The orchestra conductor has to make himself available and have an interpretation ready to communicate. Our chorus conductor had shown us a clear conception of the piece, which was great, except it bore no resemblance to the orchestra conductor's. The orchestra conductor didn't seem to know what his conception was, but it certainly wasn't what we had prepared. We're used to adjusting for differences in style and approach, but these guys were on two different planets.

We wanted to follow a leader whose vision was clear, whose conception brought the music alive. Choral singers are followers, in the best sense of the word. Not mindless automatons, but people who listen, digest, and process a wealth of information, then execute the directions as understood. Some instrumentalists say that singers have resonance where their brains should be. Oh, yeah? A church or synagogue chorister sings different sacred music every week. A symphony orchestra chorister rehearses with one conductor and performs with the orchestra's artistic director and many guest conductors. The flexibility to respond to everchanging situations requires brains.

ᖑᘎ

FOR CITIZENS of a country that begins its constitution with the words "We the people," we Americans are oddly reluctant to celebrate our followers. Oh, we erected a tomb to the unknown soldier and a memorial to those who died in Vietnam, and Aaron Copland wrote his *Fanfare for the Common Man,* but these few examples stand out against our ferocious need for charismatic leaders.

In the business world, the great leap forward of this generation was the transformation of managers into leaders—keepers of vision and motivation. Followers are only just beginning to enter the equation. A search through any business library will reward you with thousands of books on leadership, and two or three focused on followers. The InfoTrac database of articles from the business press (1980 through the present) yielded me 15,614 references to the keyword "leader" with subcategories including: training, technique, psychological aspects, research, models, methodology, measurement, management, conferences, and a scattering of others. (The magnifying glass is so sharply focused, it's a wonder business leaders don't go up in flames.) The keyword "follower" appeared in the database 132 times over the same nineteen-year period. We evidently value followers a whopping 0.8 percent as much as leaders.

In most business literature, followers are regarded as empty vessels into which the leader pours vision and energy. A dangerous assumption, as Louis XVI might have commented from the guillotine.

But most people are followers at least some of the time—no matter what their rank in the realms of business, politics, the military, or the arts. We don't like to call ourselves followers because we think of followers as passive. So pervasive is this notion of passivity that one local music critic thinks he is showering a compliment upon my chorus when he writes (as he does all too often), "The Minnesota Chorale was well-drilled." Teeth can be well drilled, sir, as can marching bands. But we are not drilled upon, nor do we drill. We sing.

In business, to avoid the stigma of passivity, we call employees team members. Some of the time, we do indeed behave with the dynamics of a team, each of us playing a specified role, passing a ball of energy and responsibility from one to another with only occasional coaching from the sidelines.

But sometimes the flow of energy flows primarily from the leader to the followers and back again. To accurately describe this situation, we must change, not the word "follower," but its connotation of bleating sheep.

What might that look like? For models at opposite ends of the followership continuum, read mysteries and pay special attention to the detective's sidekick. Dr. Watson chronicles Sherlock Holmes's cases. Archie Goodwin does the same for Nero Wolfe. But there the resemblance stops. Watson reveres Holmes. Archie refers to Wolfe as "that big, fat genius." Both Wolfe and Archie know that their success depends as much on Archie's leg work and down-to-earth perspective as on Wolfe's brilliance. Boss and employee, their mutual respect is thickly coated with cayenne pepper.

Watson acts as a sounding board, a passive role that allows Holmes to articulate his reasoning and demonstrate his superiority. On the active end of the continuum, Archie has instructions from Wolfe that when he hits an unexpected situation, he is to act "with intelligence guided by experience."

I love that phrase. For mystery writing—and life philosophy—give me Rex Stout over Sir Arthur Conan Doyle any day. When the conductor cues you wrong, when the harmonies the orchestra is playing are so bizarre you have no idea what your next note should sound like, when you're about to make a loud entrance and in that split second you realize no one else is taking a deep breath—how else can you act but with intelligence guided by experience?

Wolfe's instructions to Archie come very close to the way jurors are instructed before going into deliberation. You must find proof beyond a reasonable doubt, the judge told the jury in the criminal case on which I served. He defined that phrase as proof "such as ordinarily prudent men and women would act upon in their most important affairs"; and reasonable doubt: "based upon reason and common sense, neither fanciful doubt, nor beyond all possibility of doubt." In other words, use your intelligence guided by experience.

Archie's independence and irreverence—coupled with his passion for truth—make him what business writer Robert Kelley calls "an exemplary follower." In a 1988 *Harvard Business Review* article and in his 1992 book *The Power of Followership,* Kelley began provoking the business world with his thoughtful analysis on the art of following. We can't lose sight of those whom the leaders will lead, said Kelley. "Without his armies, after all, Napoleon was just a man with grandiose ambitions." Far from seeing the best followers as sheep, Kelley says, "What distinguishes an effective from an ineffective follower is enthusiastic, intelligent, and self-reliant participation—without star billing—in the pursuit of an organizational goal."

Ira Chaleff in his 1995 book *The Courageous Follower* takes the image of great followership further. The picture I get when most people talk about leading and following is that of a cluster of dots (the followers), connected by lines to a single leader dot off in the distance. Chaleff posits an equilateral triangle. At one corner of the base are the followers; the leader resides at the other corner of the base. At the apex of the triangle, the focus of both leader and followers, is a common purpose. "The process of clarifying purpose . . . is a critical act of strong leadership and courageous followership," says Chaleff. Leader and followers exist in those roles not because they are the boss and bossed, but because, by playing those roles well, they can best serve the common purpose.

Common purpose lies in the heart, next to religion and other matters of spirit. A betrayal of that purpose—like partying instead of learning your music—does feel like a blasphemy to those who hold the purpose dear.

Loyalty to that purpose can look like loyalty to the leader, but only as long as the leader embodies—quite literally—the common goal. "At times," says Chaleff "courageous followers need to lead from behind, breathing life into their leader's vision, or even vision into the leader's life."

∾

MOST OF US who sing in a chorus do it because we *like* following. To make music without the glory but also without the stress: no one noticing an occasional extra breath or missed note. The shade outside the limelight can feel delightful, refreshing.

Life presents human beings with one tough decision after another: "What college, what job do I go for?" "The situation with my boss (my spouse, my kid, my friend) is a complete mess. What do I do?" I consider, ponder, ask friends for advice. I hope for the best and act, then suffer or benefit from the consequences.

On days full of too many hassles after a night of too little sleep, making an insignificant choice like which route to drive home during rush hour can plunge me into grumpiness. Then I go to rehearsal, where the person on the podium has (most of the time, anyway) considered, pondered, perhaps asked for advice, and is ready to set direction. Weight lifts from my shoulders. Carrying out those directions requires skill and a host of other noble qualities, but for three hours, I am only 1/80th, 1/120th, or even 1/150th responsible.

The odd thing is that in our fractional responsibility, musicians are powerful. A French hornist I know says that you can tell how much a symphony orchestra respects a guest conductor by how high the music stands rise during rehearsal. Low music stands that offer a clear view of the baton indicate high marks for

the conductor. But watch the stands creep up as rehearsal progresses, and you are watching an orchestra tune a conductor out,
so that it can conduct itself by ear. I watched a similar process
when a guest conductor came to town last summer, substituting
for someone who had canceled. He needed a pickup chorus to
sing for free. Calls went out. Lots of calls, because this conductor
has treated every chorus in town with contempt. He got inexpe-
rienced kids who were impressed by his name.

∾

SCENE: a master class with master accompanist Martin Isepp, who
has recorded with Dame Janet Baker and a host of other extraordinary musicians.

"Why did you slow down there?" he asks the student pianist
as the soprano finishes her impassioned Schubert.

"I was following her."

Isepp leans over the keyboard. In a stage whisper, clearly
audible to the audience, he instructs: "We don't tell them. But we
never follow."

∾

I'LL TELL YOU what great followership is not. Every chorus I've
sung with as an adult has had within it a junior conductor. Junior
conductor—unlike assistant or associate conductor—is an unoffi-
cial, self-appointed post. That of pest. When that particular junior
conductor leaves, another self-appointee appears. Near as I can
tell, junior believes her job (junior is almost invariably a "her") is
to keep the conductor in line. "Joel, should we breathe between
'the' and 'earth'?" Junior knows damn well we shouldn't. Joel said
something about it last rehearsal. But a few people are still doing

it so junior helps out. The conductor may have let the mistake go this time because he figured since most people were getting it, the rest of us would pick it up. Or, he may have only enough rehearsal time to focus on some issue of greater importance. These strategic decisions a conductor makes—what to fix and what to let go—are called rehearsal technique. Conductors study it.

Junior conductors try to run the rehearsal while pretending not to. They disturb the balance of things, the sense of my job/your job. As a choral singer, my job is to execute directions—directions the conductor gives as part of his or her job. My job is no less important than the conductor's, but it *is* different.

Thinking about "my job/your job" helps me choose appropriate behavior and puts others' behavior in perspective: As a parent (or presiding grown-up), my job is to set appropriate limits and present kids with safe choices; as a kid, your job is to test those limits and make those choices. As a consultant, my job is to present recommendations; as a manager, your job is to choose a course of action and make it work. Life can get pretty unhealthy when kids rule and consultants manage.

My job/your job is an underlying assumption in our criminal justice system. As I sat listening to jury selection, I saw—not the *wheels* of justice, but a set of interlocking gears, each with its own purpose, each essential to the whole. First the judge, then the defense attorney, then the prosecutor asked potential jurors questions, ostensibly to reveal our biases, to help the lawyers determine who should not be on the jury. But, if you really listened, you could hear them teaching us the parameters of our job: "How do you feel about the narcotics laws in this country? The gun laws?"

"Too lenient," said some. "Too punitive," said others.

"Feeling as you do, could you bring in a verdict based on the laws as written, as interpreted by the judge in his final instructions?"

We got the point. We weren't there to make law. The legislators we hire when we vote do that. Or interpret the law. That's the judge's job. Or discover evidence. That's the cop's. Or present it. That's the lawyers'. We were there to give our full attention to the testimony and then decide whether there was a reasonable doubt of the defendant's guilt. That's all, and that's plenty.

For this system to work everybody has to be doing their job well including the guys who set it up. Believing in our system means believing that the presumption of innocence is a pretty good idea, and that all these interlocking gears, spinning large and small, whirling slower and faster, result, more often than not, in justice.

Similarly, a large chorus needs a conductor, not because choral singers are too weak or stupid to make music on our own, but because the end result is better music.

Following is like dancing with someone who knows how to lead. The glorious pleasures of receiving and responding, of feeling the ebb and flow of nonverbal conversation. Both partners cannot lead, but they are in constant communication. Therein lies the secret power of the follower.

Choral conductors are always yelling, "Look up! Get your nose out of the music." Of course, conductors want you watching, so you can see the cue for the ritard, and they can slow everyone down at the same rate. But conductors also need the energy from singers' eyes; when conductors receive only sound, without eye contact, they don't receive the fuel they need.

Imagine trying to create a unified splendor from forty to two hundred creatures, each possessing a unique voice, a unique life.

Perhaps an alto's son just got suspended for smoking marijuana; a bass's daughter just starred in her first ballet recital; a soprano is eight and a half months pregnant; a tenor's mother should be moved to a nursing home, but where? Death, birth, laundry, bills, carburetors, the funniest joke in years—the conductor has to make music out of it all. Give the person with the baton a break. Look up! Get your nose out of the music!

But what if you look up and get nothing back?

After dress rehearsal for our Mozart *Requiem* in Aspen, we trooped off to lunch and a few hours of rest before reassembling for the afternoon's performance. Warm-up was angry, with singers asking questions of our chorus conductor, trying to clarify and insert precision. "Is that cutoff an eighth note or a quarter note?" "How is that word pronounced in Church Latin?"

Robed in black costumes and grim faces, we marched across the lawn and filed onto the stage of the huge Music Tent. The quiet yearning of the woodwinds began, to be joined by the strings, reaching, reaching, and finally the brass, loudly asking, demanding. We took deep breaths—and began the performance of our lives.

Requiem aeternam dona eis, Domine.

It was magic. Every ounce of meaning, every drop of musicality that we could find in ourselves was there. Not mutiny—we followed his baton precisely—but transcendence. We took his lugubrious tempos and filled them with fire. There had been no discussion, no rabble-rousing, no petition signing—simply a silent, individual, and collective decision to make music. The air crackled. We gave them the Mozart *Requiem* as if it were the most precious gift in the world.

And the audience heard. They felt the significance, the connection with Mozart and with us. They let us know it, too. When it was over, they stood and cheered and beamed.

We may follow the conductor, but we serve the music. For those of us who place Wolfgang Amadeus among the heavenly host, singing dull Mozart is the greatest blasphemy of all.

Creativity's Compost

I can see them—great heaps of notes littering the place. Flat notes, unfocused notes. Eighth notes that should have been sixteenths. Notes with too much air, too little. Gorgeous notes that I held so long they traveled into the next measure and so transmuted from right notes into wrong notes. They sneak between the keys of the piano and take naps in the ancient dust on the sounding board. They snuggle together between the warm ridges of the living room radiator. They bounce on the carpet and then bury themselves between the paper clips in the desk drawer. They fly upward and augment the cobwebs. They hear my frustrated "That's not it. Again." But they don't care. When sunbeams stream through my windows they dance the Charleston with the dust motes. They settle on the cat's fur. They coagulate on my shoulders and push me down.

They don't accuse me, the mistake notes. No cutting remarks.

That I could fight. They simply pile up—hour after practice hour, day after year. Unblinking, they stare and use up my air.

And these are just wrong *notes*. What about the rest of life's mistakes? Little mistakes like putting blueberries in pancakes for consumption by a five-year-old who knows that pancakes with lumps in them are inedible, so how come you don't know? Medium errors like dropping the new puppy on his nose—twice!—because I kept forgetting that dogs are not cats. Puppies do not land on their feet when you hold them in your arms and then just let them go. And the big mistakes—oh, Lord, let's not even explore that territory. Not yet. Let's get back to musical mistakes. They're a million of them, but at least each individual is merely a tiny dot.

What should I do with these waste products of vocal production? Scrub the house! Dust, mop, sweep them into the trash and take them out Thursday night so the garbage men can haul them away Friday morning.

But wait. Standing there—tall, black, and handsome—right by the path to the garbage can—the composter. Inside its shiny container are carrot scrapings, eggshells, brown banana peels, and bits of aged, yellowed broccoli all fermenting, rotting. Maybe it's better to dispose of my mistakes there. Maybe they would get hot and bothered along with the vegetable discards, and make soil from which marvelous things grow.

∞

WRONG NOTES, false starts, ideas crossed out with blotted ink, balls of crumpled paper snowing over the floor—these crowd the lives of the creative ones: composers, painters, poets, inventors, the ones who change the world beginning in the solitude of thought.

Mistakes—bits of effort that don't work out—are as necessary to their process as air.

One discouraging day, I happened to turn the radio on, and there—years after his death—was Leonard Bernstein talking about Beethoven's rough drafts. The New York Philharmonic, in grand sonority, played attempt after attempt from Beethoven's sketchbooks. He was trying to find the right second theme for the Fifth Symphony. A toughie. What do you do after the hammer blows of *dit dit dit DAH*? A lot of what he tried to do was pretty lousy. It was so heartening to know that Beethoven wrote mediocre music. He had ordinary thoughts, came up with stupid ideas, just like the rest of us. Only mostly posterity doesn't get to hear them because he didn't stop there. He kept taking the bits that worked and playing and modifying and combining them and experimenting until the right solution emerged—the plush, almost romantic tune that would form the perfect foil to his percussive opening.

∾

IT'S ALL VERY well to talk about mistakes being necessary for creativity, but wrong notes don't kill people. Perhaps I'm taking the issue of mistakes entirely too lightly. Mistakes in hospitals kill between 44,000 and 98,000 Americans per year, according to a 1999 report from the National Academy of Sciences Institute of Medicine. That's more than the yearly tolls from highway accidents (43,450), breast cancer (42,300), or AIDS (16,500). It's the equivalent of three jumbo jets filled with patients crashing every two days. We'd probably notice that.

What the *New York Times* editorial found most shocking

about the report is not so much the numbers, as "how easy it would be to correct many of the fatal errors."

So now the forces of correction will descend—as they have with airline accidents and work-related injuries: the politicians who want to look good by keeping voters alive; the employers who would rather not pay for health care that kills their employees. My guess is they'll improve things. In the meantime, if I end up in a hospital I'm going to write down the name and color of every pill they give me and cross-check before I put it in my mouth (assuming I'm well enough to think straight). Oh, and I'll point out the correct body part to the actual surgeon who is going to cut into it.

As a society, we need to be concerned about mistakes made by doctors or airline pilots. But do those of us in other occupations need to take our own mistakes so seriously? After all, our mistakes don't kill.

∽

TWO FACES looked back at me from the bathroom mirror—mine and that of the ten-year-old sitting cross-legged in the sink. We formed a curious totem pole. I had my arms around her from behind, holding her as well as I could. She was staring at her own white face weeping, wailing, "It's all my fault!"

"What is?"

"I broke a piece off the ant farm." (It was the end of a very long tenth birthday week.)

"Is it fixable?"

"Yes."

"Well, that's probably okay then."

"But the tadpoles aren't."

"What about the tadpoles?"

"I killed them!" (tears, wails)

"How? How did you kill them?"

"Well, my grandparents gave me a frog-growing set, and you send in a card and they send you tadpoles? And I was supposed to check the mailbox every day, and I forgot for four days and when I found them they were frozen. So the tadpoles I showed you," she said to her best friend who had been invited over for this celebration, which seemed to be having its finale in the bathroom, "the tadpoles I showed you were already dead."

At the time it never occurred to me to ask what kind of idiot sends live tadpoles to Minnesota in the winter. They wouldn't last half an hour in the mailbox, let alone four days. And besides, doesn't someone at her mom's house bring in the mail every day?

At the time, I looked at the stricken face in the mirror and said, "You were supposed to check and you didn't?"

"Yeah."

"Then I guess it *is* your fault."

She looked surprised, almost relieved. I went on, "Human beings screw up. And when we do, sometimes we hurt other creatures and that's the worst screwup of all. I accidentally killed a kitten once." I did, too, and I told her about it. The kitten and I were playing inside. I was in my thirties, you understand. This isn't a kid sin I'm about to confess. So this kitten and I were getting some winter exercise running up and down the stairs when the kitten ran under my feet. I stumbled and stepped on her. She fell, trembled, and was still. Dead of internal bleeding, said the vet I rushed her to. To people who grew up on farms where cats live and die like dandelions, this incident may seem trivial. But not to this ten-year-old at that moment.

Then her friend jumped in, "Well, you know how everybody thinks my brother broke his finger because the bookcase fell on him?" Her sweet little voice was edged with competition. "Well, the bookcase fell because I pushed him into it!" Obligatory shame tinged with pride: She's a thin slip of a girl.

So then everyone went teary-eyed and smiling. The friend started to produce another True Confession, but as the presiding adult, I interrupted and said we should discuss Now What? We talked about the ant farm the birthday girl's dad had given her. And how you send in a card for the ants ("which will be shipped in six to twelve weeks, weather permitting"—smart people) and how all you can do with your big hurting mistakes is learn from them so you do better next time. Our heroine nodded and climbed down from the sink.

∾

WHAT'S A mistake anyway? At the very least, it's something that doesn't work out as planned. An error can be innocuous, but a mistake hurts somebody in some way. The content might be the same, but not the consequences. Take a slip of the pencil on an arithmetic problem: for a second grader, the error knocks off a couple of points on an overall score; for an aerospace engineer, the mistake can cause a rocket to explode.

There's an overlap with sin, I'm sure. But it seems to me that sin is defined by others: It has not only a religious but an official ring. I decide what choices in my life are mistakes.

A useful idea that can be borrowed from sin is that of omission and commission. My mistakes of commission don't haunt me years later. By then, I can often see the good that came out of the disastrous job, the failed marriage.

I was talking to a friend the other day—a business consultant and practitioner of Zen—about the clients whose business we each seek, and the clients we'll never work for again. He said, "Yes, by the time I was forty I had developed one of the great philosophies of my life: 'Avoid assholes.' "

To avoid them, you have to recognize them from a distance, and that takes a few collisions. Me, I've collided with jerks of all sizes, shapes, genders, and races—and good guys, as well. I've learned that you can't trust someone just because she's female, or reminds you of your sister. Useful experience, those collisions.

The mistakes on which I spend the most regret are two kinds of omission: simple omission and complicity.

I chose not to attend my sister's second wedding. I'll probably regret that omission for the rest of my life.

And then there were the times I let someone trespass on my soul. My belly hurt so much I could see an invisible knife sticking out of it, but it took me forever to realize the someone might have thrust it there while I was looking into his face with deep, needy eyes. I finally tired of adding self-chastisement to emotional cuts and bruises, and I forged, from hard, glowing steel, a small round shield called NO. I carry it with me ready to be placed in front of my belly—before, rather than after the attack.

No, you may not tell me what to feel. No, you may not do hurtful things and then tell me it was my fault because I didn't love you enough. No, you may not define me. No, I will not allow your insults inside me. They're yours. They bounce right off my shield.

Yes, I will live my life, make my choices, deal with the consequences. Yes, I know that when you laugh at the assholes they get very worried. Yes, there is kindness and bravery everywhere. Yes, you make mistakes and so do I, so let's draw our courage about us and begin again.

Like refrains from well-loved songs, our mistakes visit us again and again:

"Of course I have learned from my mistakes. I can repeat them precisely." I heard that years ago coming from my radio. It was a broadcast of the "Goon Show," I believe.

A mistake that you make over and over is called a character flaw. Flaws are found in people and designs and jewels.

"You know why Geoffrey dumped you, don't you?" asked one of his good friends.

"No," I sobbed.

"You're available," she said. "Geoffrey never falls in love with available women."

Me, aged twelve, to Mom: "I'm never going to make the same mistake twice."

Mom, smiling a funny smile: "That's good to wish for, but don't be too sad if you're wrong."

Choreographer Jimmy Waring to his class of teenage dancers: "I'm bored with your mistakes. You make the same ones, over and over, each of you. The same mistakes. Trade them!"

∞

OUR MISTAKES can feel so bad. What if we could compost them—transform them into nourishment? How might such a composting process work?

Compost heaps come in all shapes and characters—like the

neighbors who create them. Anne has the deluxe black plastic kind, from the rich person's garden catalog. She would have employed a less expensive method, but our landlord insisted that the compost be raccoon-proof, so black plastic it was. It looks like a garbage can with vents. You just put scraps in, wait a year and voilà! good, rich garden dirt. The gardening books call this the "no work" or the "slow, cool, passive" method.

Anne is not a rich person, but rather a playwright who dresses up for her day job by brushing her hair. Nor is she a gardener. She just can't bear to throw away useful material, whether orange peels or bits of dialog. The people and events in her life have a way of reappearing as characters and scenes.

Tom was at the other end of the compost continuum, the end I call Boys Who Love Playing in the Dirt (I don't know any females who are this far gone, although I'm sure there are some). His compost heap lay open, a mountain of scraps at one end of the garden. In the summer, he would gleefully head out, shoeless, pitchfork in hand, to lift and turn, sweating under the sun, smelling all that activity. One year, Tom acquired a load of manure from a farmer to add to this. "Guess what I've got!" he shouted as he drove his pickup into the driveway, his face alight. It wasn't difficult.

With compost, Tom built a garden that took up three-fourths of his city lot: carrots, potatoes, broccoli, purple string beans ("because they're easier to find when you pick") all the borders trimmed with flowers. The soil when he first got there was mostly clay. A family of mice made a nest in the compost one winter, safe from the twenty-below cold. My cat sat by the compost hour after hour, hoping for a mouse appearance.

Then the lot got too shady. Tom and his girlfriend broke up. So he sold the house and headed out into the world in his trusty

red Ford pickup, leaving behind the most fertile earth in the
neighborhood.

∾

I PONDER mistakes because way down deep where I keep my
beliefs that probably aren't true and certainly aren't mature, I
think if I could only figure this out I wouldn't fall off my bicycle
and still ache months later or do thoughtless harm to the people I
love or stumble over a kitten and watch it die. If I didn't make
mistakes, life wouldn't hurt so damn much.

Then I tell myself not to worry about mistakes because I'm
going to make them, so why worry about the inevitable. But time,
time is awasting. I find myself at middle age smarter about a million things I don't do anymore. By the time you understand how
to parent your five-year-old she's fifteen and by the time you really understand your job they've sold the company or promoted or
fired or retired you. You can stand as still as you like, but it won't
stop the ground from shifting under you. Then, of course, standing still becomes a mistake.

I'll never get it right, not all of it, all the time. I know that. But
what if all these mistakes were making something useful out of
me? I think of Tom's legacy to the neighborhood, that rich plot of
earth. No one is planting on it now because the trees are too thick.
But maybe someday someone will make a patch of sunshine and
grow a surprisingly beautiful garden because Tom bought home a
load of shit one day.

∾

WALKING TO rehearsal one evening, I fell into step beside a member of the Minnesota Orchestra's percussion department. "When

bored in the symphony, watch the timpani": that's what my father taught me—he who loves Broadway more than Bach. So I did—whenever I didn't have to watch the conductor—I watched the timpani and the cymbals, chimes, snare drums, wood blocks, ratchets, and once the branch of a tree being scratched against the wall of Orchestra Hall. Now I'd been given a moment with one of those magicians of noise to ask the percussion question that had always troubled me: "Isn't it awfully stressful? I mean, if the cymbals come in at the wrong place, everybody knows."

He shrugged, this little guy with a wiry body, hooked nose, and gray hair where there was hair, "Yeah, but what are they going to do? Shoot you?"

∽

MORE THAN your choice of career or spouse, your preferred genre of mistakes will define you. A soprano soloist uncertain of her entrance will usually jump in. Better an early entrance than to be found missing. A bass in the chorus, on the other hand, will hold back, afraid of making himself conspicuous with an unpaid solo. (Of course, if the whole section holds back, the conductor will find the missed entrance quite conspicuous.)

What kinds of mistakes do you make? Do you err on the side of jumping into possibility when life beckons? Or do you hold back until conditions are definitely favorable? Are you more afraid of not following your heart's dream or spending your old age bagging groceries?

The choice of mistake will define a business, too. Take 3M. This reputed paragon of innovation was born out of a whopping mistake. Minnesota Mining and Manufacturing has never really lived up to its middle name. These days they mine rock for roofing shingles—a minute particle of the overall business. But back in 1902 in Two Harbors, Minnesota, a group of five businessmen thought that mining was going to be a big part of their baby company. They planned to build industrial grinding wheels which used an abrasive called corundum. They acquired what they thought was a deposit of the stuff. A post-purchase check revealed it was nothing of the sort. (At this point two shares of 3M stock were trading for one shot of whiskey in the local bar.) The founders took stock. Inventory: useless minerals plus knowledge about abrasives and adhesives. So? Dump the minerals, buy abrasives elsewhere, and start manufacturing sandpaper (which is made by using adhesives to coat paper with abrasives). The little company did not die. Opinion regarding whether it lives happily ever after or not depends on which employee you talk to on which day, but I sure wish I had shelled out a couple of shots of whiskey, since 1999 sales were nearly $16 billion.

Mistakes that spur creativity were on the mind of the patron saint of 3M, William McKnight, when he issued his 1941 "McKnight Principles." He held that the mistakes made by innovative employees do less damage than the mistakes dictatorial management makes when it squashes individual initiative.

Does the company live by this? Sometimes. The Principles gave my friend Jane backup support of biblical proportions when she was getting pummeled for spending her department's yearly budget on a project of great creativity and limited success.

But if mistakes are acceptable, what happens to quality? This seems to me an essential dilemma in every field of human endeavor—business, health care, the arts, sports. How do we reconcile Mr. McKnight with quality theory's goal of "zero tolerance for errors"? I consulted with Denny Nowlin, a loyal and resilient

3Mer. He dug out a manual from an innovation program he had worked on in the eighties. Two sentences leaped out at me: "Original mistakes . . . really cannot be avoided if the venture is sufficiently innovative . . . This is not a tolerance for shoddy work." I love the phrase "shoddy work," and its disdain for inferior craftsmanship. The two sentences exactly described the paradox we were grappling with, but offered no resolution.

Denny has spent a lot of time catching people in the halls and the cafeteria, asking, "What's a good mistake, a high-quality mistake?" From their answers, he assembled a picture of something he calls a "productive mistake." A productive mistake is: (1) made in the service of mission and vision; (2) acknowledged as a mistake; (3) learned from; (4) considered valuable; (5) shared for the benefit of all.

These criteria don't sound difficult until you consider actually doing them. If I take the idea of productive mistakes personally, the implications take my breath away. I have to know my mission—the unique contribution I'm trying to make during my time on Earth. My choices must be consonant with that intention. I've got to take responsibility for my choices, whether the results are positive or negative. I have to think about what I did wrong, and figure out what I'm going to do differently next time. Although I take responsibility, I can't wallow in shame, because that's not productive. I have to tell what I've learned to others, even if it makes me look like a fool.

Denny's criteria for productive mistakes are, in fact, a mistake-composting process—a process that creates the nourishment we call collective wisdom.

Shortly after our discussions in 1994, Denny's department was eliminated. The people were given a choice—a severance package or placement on the "unassigned list," a sort of employee recycling program, where you get a desk and a phone and salary for several months while you look for a job within the company.

Productive mistakes never became official company policy. These days, 3M prefers to talk about innovation through intention rather than happenstance. But I'm not overly discouraged. The idea may be lying underground, while political storms and reorganizations rage overhead, safely waiting to bloom again.

∾

PRODUCTIVE mistakes assume we can learn from other people's mistakes. I believe we can, but only if we're willing to relinquish our beloved sense of superiority. It's hard to watch for banana peels in your path when you're pointing and laughing at some other slob who just slipped and hit the pavement.

What about preventing others' mistakes? If I see my friend step in front of a speeding car, I grab her jacket and pull her back. But can I pull my other friend out of harm's way, the one who's fallen in love with a superficial, selfish woman? Probably not, and he won't thank me for trying.

∾

WE DON'T allow mistakes on classical recordings—at least not obvious ones. Did the flute miss his entrance? Take it again. Did the girls choir gradually sink a half step from beginning to end? Tell the computerized editing system to poke the pitch up gradually. "In all the recordings I've made," a conductor told me, "no producer has ever said 'Would you take it again, please? That phrase wasn't musical.' They focus on the obvious mistakes, the ones that no one can challenge them on. The critics are like that, too. There's no risk in saying the B-flat is too flat."

Yet what is one flat note when compared to a lifeless performance?

∾

I HAVE experienced composted mistakes, so I know it's possible— at least in music. There's a song by Vaughan Williams, "Silent Noon." I've worked on it off and on for years. At the end, you jump up an octave from the word "the" to "song," holding the high note, getting softer and more tender, so that when you descend to finish the phrase with "of love," the love is already there.

Those four notes used to be so difficult—either I didn't get soft enough or the sound disappeared completely. I pulled out the music and sang it through the other day. The phrase simply fell into place. I haven't practiced it in at least two years, and somehow it got easy all by itself.

∾

SOME MISTAKES refuse to stay mistakes.

1924. George Gershwin writes a melody that he intends to use as the verse for a song. George and Ira (lyricist and brother) decide that the melody is too strong and insistent to use as a verse. (The tune is similar to the first theme of George's "Rhapsody in Blue," which has recently premiered to great popular success.) It would overpower the rest of the song, so they drop it from both the song and whatever show they were working on at the time.

The Gershwin brothers begin working on their first complete Broadway score together, *Lady, Be Good!* starring Fred and Adele Astaire. They decide to resurrect the rejected tune. Thinking about the situation in which Adele's character finds herself, Ira writes

Someday he'll come along
The man I love.

The song helps obtain financing for the show. On a ship returning to New York from London (where George had been working on another production), George plays "The Man I Love" for banker Otto Kahn. When asked to back *Lady, Be Good!* Kahn initially refuses. But when informed that "The Man I Love" is in the score, Kahn decides to invest $10,000. *Lady, Be Good!* turns out to be one of the few shows that ever returned Kahn's investment, according to Deena Rosenberg, in her book *Fascinating Rhythm*. Yet the song that clinched the deal—the song George said he wrote "for young girls sitting on fire escapes on hot summer nights in New York and dreaming of love"—was pulled one week into the Philadelphia tryout. Adele Astaire was the embodiment of a frivolous flapper; she couldn't pull off its mood of wistful longing. So the song was rejected for show number two. Ah well, off to the compost heap.

"The Man I Love" disappeared from *Lady, Be Good!* but the sheet music had been printed to sell in the theater lobby during out-of-town tryouts. One Lady Mountbatten liked it so much, she asked George for an autographed copy. Taking it home to London, she gave it to her favorite dance band. Other bands in London and Paris began playing it as well.

It's now 1927. Back in New York, the Gershwins put "The

Man I Love" into their show *Strike Up the Band,* a grim satire about war, with a book by George S. Kaufman. Rosenberg writes of its being sung as a duet. Maybe that was in the Long Branch, New Jersey, tryout. Alec Wilder, in his *American Popular Song,* says that in the Philadelphia tryout Morton Downey sang a male version—"The Girl I Love." The song remained in the show, but the show folded.

Perhaps it might work in yet a fourth show, *Rosalie.* Ira Gershwin rewrote the lyrics at least twice but didn't recall ever hearing it rehearsed. Cut again.

1930. *Strike Up the Band* is rewritten and revived to enthusiastic response. But "The Man I Love" is dropped again—this time *before* tryouts. The great American singer Helen Morgan had taken it up, and it had become so popular independently that the show's creators felt it could no longer be effectively integrated into a musical.

This complete failure of a show tune has been called the most moving popular song of our time. It is also pivotal in the history of American theater songs. "The Man I Love" took us from the witty frivolity of the twenties to deeper emotions—songs that combine longing, introspection, and sometimes irony: The Gershwins went on to give us the poignancy of "They're writing songs of love / but not for me." Rodgers and Hart wrote "Falling in love with love is falling for make-believe." Cole Porter's "Begin the Beguine," Duke and Harburg's "April in Paris"—as Rosenberg points out, these and so many other great songs owe a debt to "The Man I Love."

You and I might never have heard it, if Lady Mountbatten hadn't asked for that sheet music.

Now, the great Broadway composers were all frugal recyclers.

A tune cut from one show often became a hit in the next. But "The Man I Love" persisted long after most songs would have given up. Throughout its convoluted gestation period, when all the Gershwins' efforts with it seemed to fail, the song insisted on being born.

∾

IN THIS LIFE we make the best mistakes we know how to make. Then, with any luck, we go out and make new ones. I don't make mistakes when I watch TV or take a walk. These activities are pleasant, restful. But I could not make a life of them. After all, the easiest way to avoid wrong notes is to never open your mouth and sing. What a mistake that would be.

Quartet Making

"*H*ow many sopranos does it take to screw in a lightbulb?" asked Liz, as we exited the Denver airport and sped toward Aspen.

"How many?" we dutifully sang out, excited to be on our way to a week of singing and rehearsals, without job or family responsibilities.

"Three. One to screw it in. One to pull the ladder out from under her. And one to say 'I could have done it better than that!'"

Oh, dear. Are singers really as mean-spirited as that? I thought. Here I was, committed to practically sitting in these women's laps for seven straight days.

∾

MY FEARS had begun during rehearsal two months before, when our personnel manager had announced, "About the Aspen Music

Festival. The Chorale won't be supplying transportation to take you to Aspen from the Denver airport and to ferry you to and from rehearsals. You can take city buses, but their schedule doesn't often coincide with ours. I suggest you form carpools and get the best deal on a car rental that you can."

Ah, the costs of being an unpaid singer performing at one of the world's great music festivals in one of the world's richest resorts. The airfare was cheap, the good people in the neighboring resort of Snowmass had donated condos for our lodging. But meals and wheels were up to us.

A carpool. The realization hit that I had spent every Monday night over the last four or five years singing with the same people—more or less—and had made no friends. None. I had once felt pity for a pianist who spoke of spending four years at Juilliard and graduating without a single friend. I figured it must be Juilliard. No point in making friends with those who played your instrument: They were probably after your place in the orchestra, or competing for the prize money you so desperately needed. And besides, when you're practicing eight hours a day in addition to attending classes, who has time to socialize?

But here was I—an amateur chorister—in the same predicament. Could it be that music is unfriendly? Oh, I had acquaintances in my chorus, but largely among the altos—more specifically the *short* altos I stand next to when we sing. Mere acquaintances, though. During our weekly fifteen-minute rehearsal break, we certainly hadn't grown close. And I hadn't ventured out of the alto section much. I would find myself awash with a cocktail-party shyness at the thought of walking up to these strangers—the tenors, basses, and sopranos I'd been making music with moments before—and making small talk.

But I needed a carpool. I gathered my courage and approached Chris (Alto II, 5'1"). She consulted with Sandra (Alto II, 5'3"), her roommate for the trip. Sandra said "Sure," and broke the short-alto apartheid by suggesting Liz, a soprano, who is almost 5'4" when she stands very tall. Carpool complete.

∞

THE COLORADO road snaked its way through mountains clean and tall. You could see wildflowers out the windows, a winding river tumbling over itself as it rushed downhill—and, at least if you were Liz, you spotted a discount mall.

"Should we go?" she asked, with a gleam in her eye like that of a kid on the first day of vacation heading for an ice-cream shop.

"Oo, let's," said Sandra.

"We might be late to rehearsal," cautioned Chris.

"Oh, let's do it anyway," I said, defying my performer's conscience.

Forty-five minutes later, the compact rental car was further compacted by shopping bags crammed in between singers, suitcases, snacks, and the water bottles we vocalists carried everywhere long before the rest of America picked up the custom.

We got silly. Someone started singing "Doo wah diddy diddy dum diddy doo." Not my repertoire, but I could certainly sing the refrain. I countered with something from the *Rodgers and Hart Songbook*. The others hummed backup.

We began to get to know one another. Two monied, two not. Two thin, two not. Two married, two not. Three brown heads of hair (one dyed), and one halo of silver.

Chris buttons the top button of her shirts. Her pants are pressed. Her sweater is neatly draped over her shoulders. A city lady, surely. But, as we discovered during the hour that we passed inquiring into The Life of Chris, she never goes anywhere without a compass and binoculars. She strained the ligaments in her arms hauling buckets of water when she was in charge of cooking for Outward Bound in northern Minnesota. Then she moved to St. Paul and began working as a neighborhood organizer, a job that involved endless grant proposals and evening meetings. Her speaking voice and singing voice are rich, low, round, dark. "Well, I'm not really sure," she would say, elongating the "oo" in "sure" and sliding the pitch a bit.

Sandra has prematurely silver hair, brilliant blue eyes, and a hoarse, wonderful, Marlene Dietrich voice. Her eyes really look at you; her voice surrounds you, warm and charming. She can talk one minute about the hundreds of thousands of dollars involved in moving her consulting business and the next minute gasp, "My ears! I forgot my earrings! I'm naked. I can't go!"

Liz has the voice of a flute laughing, which she does, a lot. She loves to talk, and interrupts with great good will. Brown hair, brown eyes, dimples, plump. She quit working as a real estate broker when her husband sold his business for millions. She sits on boards of directors, works for the League of Women Voters, and runs a kind of family bed and breakfast at the four-bedroom, centrally heated, "cabin" up north. She answers the question "What do you do?" with "community volunteer," so people often underestimate her. At the end of our first meal together, she pulled out a calculator capable of statistical analysis (used to calculate mortgage payments in her previous career) and announced our correct amounts.

And me, the writer and second soprano turned alto after two bouts of laryngitis, masking my insecurity with a persona of New

York opinionated. No one can believe it at our first dinner when I—the Joan who seems so sure of herself—call the waitress back three times: "Decaf." "No, red wine." "No, sorry, really, decaf."

For one week in Aspen that rented car became a kind of commuter boat—isolated and intimate—as it ferried us down from our quarters on Snowmass Mountain, across the valley, up to rehearsals and performances in Aspen, and then back again.

We talked shop: "How much do you practice?" "Who do you study with?" "What do you think of the guest conductor?" And we commiserated in all the well-worn phrases: "I know, I know" and "Good for you." We zoomed to rehearsal together, hiked the Maroon Bells mountains, talked incessantly, made ourselves conspicuous in restaurants: When the staff began singing "Happy Birthday" to anyone at all, we chimed in with extravagant, four-part harmony.

We attended concerts, too:

"That cellist." (sigh) "The way he *listened* to the pianist."

"With the back of his head."

"Through the skin of his arms."

Silence. Each of us remembering—in our bodies—the quality of that listening and how it infused the sound. If you'd asked us later who said which part of the thought, no one would have known.

∾

MUSIC BRINGS with it not only bonding but envy. Tiny Chris has a big, dark, rich alto sound. When the orchestra conductor requested a small chorus of the better singers, our staff conductor always chose Chris, but usually not me, even though I practice more than she does. I accept it, but I don't like it.

Liz is a *real* soprano. She can place those high notes with just the right amount of air so they spinspinspin and move with the focus of a light beam, always soft, always traveling, never stuck. Impressive. Annoying.

Liz and Chris have VOICES.

Sandra and I have VOICES—we're choral utility players. But Sandra speaks German fluently, her French is competent, and her Mandarin gets her by in China. I can *pronounce* many languages, and ask a French baker to hand me a loaf of bread, but when Parisians start talking politics—even American politics—I'm lost.

So I envied them all. And I loved them all. Because we laughed, God how we laughed. About conductors who are unprepared, about the tenor many thought was gay who emphatically wasn't, about the men and the lack of men in our lives.

The day before our final performance we had planned a sightseeing expedition. I woke up early, went out of the hotel door to the hot tub, and stood there, in the steam of the cold morning, looking down the green slope of the mountain, watching hot air balloons rise—silent, fabulous, gaudy as Christmas tree ornaments—and I knew I wasn't going anywhere that day. I couldn't listen to another ounce of musical chatter. I slipped a note under Liz's door. "I'm feeling really tired and my throat's a bit sore, so I'm going to take a relaxing solo day. Have a great time."

I meant, "I love you all dearly and if I spend any time with you today, I'll scream and froth at the mouth." But I've acquired a habit of timidity from an outside world that finds a need for solitude offensive and vaguely threatening. I didn't need to hedge with this group. Their individual generosity allowed each of us to be who we are. Besides, I'd trained them during the week. We'd get to a restaurant and find a twenty-minute wait for a table. I'd say "See you." "Fine," they would nod. I'd wander off, feeling the balm of solitude sink into my skin. They'd have a convivial drink. We'd reassemble for dinner, relaxed and content.

Phrases like "She's not a team player" or "We're all a family, and families should be together" were just not a part of this quartet's vocabulary. Once reunited, our stories and jokes burbled like a mountain brook. Sentences swooped over and under one another, punctuated by laughter—delighted, rueful, malicious. A joyful noise.

Outsiders find it hard to understand how we can all talk at once and still hear each other. "Multiplexing!" I explained later when I met Sandra's engineer husband. "But how can you receive and transmit at the same time?" he asked. And the truth is, we don't. Chris and I will be talking about something and Liz will be so excited by her own idea about it that she jumps in. Chris and I half hear what she says, but neither of us is going to be interrupted, so we finish what we were saying. Meanwhile, Sandra is interested in Liz's perspective and starts to chat with Liz about it, so that when Chris and I are finished, we simply shift to the other conversation already in progress.

Theme, countertheme, transposition, variation. It worked for Bach.

But what are the themes of friendship? A time, a place, a particular set of individuals—what was it about this combination that worked and kept on working long after the initial event was gone? It made me think about all the friendships in my life, and how I take them too much for granted—me and the rest of society.

Yards of relationship books fill bookstore shelves: how to get a lover, how to be a better lover, how to be a better parent, how to take care of your elderly parents. Where are the popular books on how to be a good friend?

"I don't know who discovered water," said Marshall McLuhan, "But I'm pretty sure it wasn't the fish." Like McLuhan's finny creatures, we spend our days swimming in an ocean of friendships—mostly oblivious, because mostly our friendships work. We get along. That's why we're friends. The very ease that makes friendship so valuable makes it largely invisible.

This friendship began with singing. Every friendship has at least one currency—one medium of exchange. You can see this most clearly in single-currency friendships. You play golf. You discover someone who plays at about the same level of skill, and can also take Tuesday mornings off. So each Tuesday, one of you picks the other up and off you go. You chat, you enjoy each other's company. You play well some days. Other days you strive to reach mediocrity. Tuesday morning golf anchors your week. You arrange your life around it. Your family, your coworkers, everyone knows your routine. Then your friend's arthritis gets so bad that she has to stop. For a few weeks, you get together for breakfast on Tuesday mornings instead, but it feels awkward. The conversation that flowed so easily when you were striding over a grass carpet, stumbles and halts when you're sitting and eating. No reason that you can pinpoint. You find yourself working to come up with topics, and you never used to have to do that.

An acquaintance calls to see if you'd like to play Tuesday morning.

"I'll have to get back to you," you say. You call your former golf buddy: "Would you mind if I . . . ?" Her sigh of relief is audible. She'd really like to use that time to get together with an acquaintance of hers who's also contemplating knee replacement surgery.

The odd thing about single-currency friendships is they can

feel so close when you're in them. There you are—toiling away at the project at work, or the college reunion, or the League of Women Voters state debates, or the amateur musical. People who hardly know one another coalesce into something much richer than acquaintances. You acknowledge your strengths and weaknesses: "Oh, I'd be no good at that piece, but I could take on that other job." You get creative about problem solving: "Well, I can't take on that first piece either, but here's a way we can work around it, and I'll take responsibility for that." Together, you find resources that no single individual considered before: "My brother-in-law's best friend can help us with that."

You work and you accomplish. And when the event takes place, you celebrate and bask in the warm glow of appreciating each other.

And then, more often than not, everyone goes back to his or her life. If you had taken them into your heart as friends, you're in for an icy shock. These are single-currency friends, situational friends, bonded by a particular time, place, and task.

Maybe it's more than the ending of a single event. Maybe, like the former golf buddy, one person's life situation changes. The woman you cleaved to in the divorce support group remarries. The best buddy in your army unit returns to his family thousands of miles from you. One person's currency remains dollars, but the other has converted to yen. The friendship dissolves.

Single-currency friendships may not always endure, but they can be immensely important. Take neighbors: proximity is the currency. I enjoyed chatting with Vern when he lived upstairs from me. When he moved away I didn't miss him a bit. But one night, when we were still neighbors, I fell and smashed up my face and couldn't lift my head without vomiting. I called Vern to help me sit up. Vern insisted I needed a doctor and called the ambulance. Later he called the emergency room to let me know he'd cleaned up the blood and puke from the bathroom so I wouldn't have to come home to it, and that if I were going to be staying in the hospital he'd take care of the cat.

Any neighbor would call an ambulance. But cleaning up the mess—that is friendship of a high order.

Proximity is a fragile currency. Do you encounter each other every day or two on the sidewalk, or every month or two when mowing your respective back lawns? When I lived next door to Judy and Steve, they would invite me into their family for dinner once in a while. Then I moved across the alley. We no longer lived side by side, but rather back-to-back. The invitations stopped. It would have required picking up a phone. If the last name you mentally assign a neighbor has to do with location (Judy and Steve NextDoor or Ellen and Ed OnTheCorner) you can be fairly certain you have a single-currency relationship. (The same is true of Steve InAccountsPayable or Sally TheMarketingVP'sAssistant.)

As the number of currencies increases, so does the richness of the friendship, and its ability to endure. In Aspen, we began with proximity and music. Music making combined with social time provides something that neither ordinary friendship nor collegiality do anymore. In our business lives, we have stripped away formality, in a weird imitation of friendship. We have casual Friday. We call each other by first names. But we are not friends, and woe betide the person who forgets that. We work together, we even create together sometimes, but when someone's head has to roll, we would just as soon it was the person at the desk next to ours. Many of us enjoy our colleagues but don't really trust them.

What's lacking in friendship, on the other hand, is that we do not work together. We socialize. We share our tribulations, our feelings, and (those of us in the therapized generations) our feelings about our feelings. We play together. But we do not raise barns. We help each other move, until aging backs and knees start giving out. We do good works, like cooking for a friend who's going through chemotherapy. But that's about it. And how can you really know someone until you have collectively created something more important than either of you?

The quartet's residence at the Aspen Music Festival was gone in a week and we remain friends a decade later. All four of us wine, dine, chatter, and laugh, perhaps only a half dozen times a year, but each time is a joyous milestone. After we left Aspen, we lost the currency of proximity, but we still had music (at least for the next few years) and we discovered another currency that had been deep at work all along: "You know what I mean." The laughter that comes from getting the point instantly—the intellectual point with all its emotional implications—confers resilience— a resilience that we were going to need to make the transition from first-degree to second-degree friends.

First-degree friends call *you* to ask: "How was the audition, the presentation, the test, the blind date, the first encounter with the in-laws?" First-degree friends may not remember each other's birthday (that's another sort of skill) but they know what's up next on the friend's life agenda. You wake up Tuesday wondering if it's going to be cold enough to wear your new wool sweater, and conscious that your friend's biopsy is scheduled for 10:00 A.M. Her life is at least as much a part of your life as the weather. You talk or get together often enough that your first-degree friend can ask, "How are you?" rather than, "How have you been?"

First-degree friends know when you're out of town. If your first-degree friends can't get ahold of you for several days, they'll check up on you. They know you're not traveling, so something might be wrong. For safety's sake, people living alone need at least one first-degree friend. If you're a single person who aspires to mental health, you have to have someone in your life who will notice if you don't return a call in twenty-four hours.

Second-degree friends may also be soulmates, but you're in touch only every few weeks or months. Second-degree friends have to ask "How have you been?" But when you answer, they understand immediately and fully. First- and second-degree friends get it, whatever "it" is. They respond in a way that feels right—sometimes with words, sometimes behavior. In an emergency, they'll drop everything to be there.

You're glad to have third-degree friends in your circle of acquaintances. You see them from time to time, enjoy their company, but feel no loss when they move away or fade away.

A shift in degree may destroy friendship, bringing with it grief that is neither recognized nor honored in our society: The best friend who used to live two doors down moves a thousand miles away or even just across town. You don't drop by anymore. You make appointments to see each other. You have to use some mechanical means of transport. The texture of your days suffers. Or a friend marries someone mean. Or another friend marries someone wonderful and doesn't need to talk with you every other day. There, in his bedroom, is all the companionship he wants right now. This is one reason many of us find weddings sad. For many people a spouse is the primary, maybe the only, first-degree friend. Maybe the newly married person and his old first-degree buddy will be able to build a second-degree friendship, but maybe not.

I couldn't. I'm delighted with Jim's bride—strong, compassionate, wise, silly on occasion—I couldn't have ordered up a better match for him. But when Jim and I stopped calling each other every day or two, the whole thing fell apart. "How have you been?" felt awkward as hell. I miss him.

The hurt astonishes, because your friendship was so ordinary. As if the moon said "Half is good enough for you. No more full moons."

Even friendships many degrees distant have significance. My friend Jane knows the name of the man who comes by her cubicle after five and empties her wastebasket into his huge gray plastic garbage can. He may be a twenty-fifth degree friend, but she works late and he's there, part of the fabric of her evenings, so Jane, being Jane, knows his name.

This is one of many reasons that moving—even a few miles—can be wrenching. The postal carrier, the café worker who remembers that you like your latte with skim milk, the familiar face at the teller's window of your local branch—all these nth-degree friends that you don't make appointments to see—gone. The loss is significant and usually unacknowledged.

During that one week in Aspen, the four of us became first-degree friends. We returned home and floated out to the second-degree. There we have stayed, year after year. Amazing.

∽

MAYBE I could find a wealth of songs to give me insight into the nature of this friendship, I thought, and the nature of friendship itself.

The Beatles got by "with a little help from" their friends. Cole Porter wrote about "friendship, friendship / just the perfect blend-ship." Pete Seeger and Arlo Guthrie created an album—*Precious Friend*—that I had to buy on CD because I wore my cassettes to shreds. There are a handful more that we could probably bring to mind, if we sat down and thought about it. But it's clear that in pop music, lovers outnumber friends in ways beyond measuring. So what about classical?

The choral symphonies—Beethoven's Ninth, Mahler's Second and Eighth—focus on joy, God, death, redemption. Big stuff, heavy stuff. That's when the symphony composers bring in the choral cast of thousands.

Then there is that other great chunk of music for orchestra and chorus—the oratorios. When composers like Handel, Haydn, and Mendelssohn picked stories, they chose the Cecil B. DeMille–size biblical tales: the prophet Elijah's struggles with the followers of a pagan god, the creation of the world, the story of the Messiah from birth to resurrection. Nowhere in their music do you find the smaller-scale stories, though they exist in Scripture—like the moment of friendship and loyalty when Ruth turns to her mother-in-law Naomi and says "Whither thou goest I will go."

Carl Orff wrote the most secular of choral music in *Carmina Burana* and *Catulli Carmina*. In the first, he has the men sing an ode to drinking; and in the second, Roman teenagers (of both sexes) sing their appreciation of specific portions of each others' anatomies. (Yes, that's what's happening when the translation disappears for a few lines in the concert program or CD insert.) But even Orff's people do not sing about friendship.

My quest for friendship music progresses to the solo repertoire. I could easily bring to mind arias and art songs about requited love, unrequited love, love of spring and nightingales, love of God, cruel love, faithful love, mother love, and even father love.

But no love of a friend. Maybe it was just my limited knowledge. So I sent out word to friends, and friends of friends, and electronic acquaintances of friends.

The opera buffs weighed in. "What about *La Bohème*?" asked Liz. The artists hang out together in their favorite café as if it were some nineteenth-century *Cheers*. In act 1, when the musician Schaunard actually acquires money, his first thought is to buy food and wine to share with his fellow Bohemians. Most touching of all, in act 4 the philosopher Colline sells his overcoat to buy medicine for his pal Rodolfo's girlfriend, the dying Mimì. These men are *friends,* facing life together, sharing what little they have, rejoicing and mourning together. But the only time anyone actually sings about friendship is when Colline sweetly bids farewell to his "faithful friend," the overcoat.

My correspondents led me to few operatic characters who sing directly about their friendship. In Bizet's *Pearl Fishers*, two men proclaim their undying loyalty to one another in the first act, so that one can betray the other by the third act—for the love of the virgin priestess.

Verdi's Don Carlo and his friend Rodrigo also proclaim their friendship early on. Later, Rodrigo chooses to die so that his friend can live and lead Flanders to freedom. Melodramatic, sure. But Rodrigo's sacrifice touched my heart more deeply than Don Carlo's doomed (and much expressed) passion for his stepmother, Elisabeth.

Still, the little friendship music I found in opera speaks too grandly for me. My concern lies less in dying for my friends than living in good-humored company with them.

"Eureka!" cried a German lieder aficionado, "I found a couple!" "To a Dead Friend's Drinking Glass," Schumann sadly serenades. Schubert set a poem by Alois Zettler lauding friends and wine equally. The singer wouldn't want to live without them, or die either, unless they have preceded him to heaven.

A professor in Colorado put thumbs down on chansons: "I know the French repertory well and can't think of any songs that deal with friendship (as opposed to erotic or besmitten love)."

There are probably more examples than those I unearthed with my informal survey, but I bet there aren't many. Why so many love songs and so few songs about friendship? I pondered for a long time whether it might have something to do with the male gender of most poets whose words were set to music. Standing shoulder to shoulder facing the world is a more traditional male image, while looking into each other's eyes and talking about "our relationship" seems more like female friends. The shoulder-to-shoulder guys are more likely to sing about what they're facing than about each other.

My lieder aficionado friend blames the lack of friendship songs on the Romantic sensibility—poets writing about the unattainable ideal or the unique ecstatic experience. "After all," he said, "even when they were writing about love, the Romantics didn't write about the pleasure of having breakfast with the same person for twenty-five years."

Both reasons contribute, I suspect. But stronger than either is that friendship is the relationship we want to take for granted, the easy relationship we can rely on when our love lives become messy and painful.

Still, I thought, there must be some classical composer, somewhere, who wrote about friendship in a way that would speak to me. Then I came upon Samuel Barber's monk and cat.

Pangur, white Pangur,

wrote the eighth- or ninth-century monk, probably scribbling in the margins of a manuscript he was inscribing.

The piano rolls along with a three pulse 1-2-3, 2-2-3, 3-2-3. The voice, on the other hand, is mostly in two: 1-2, 2-2. But both are flowing so smoothly that the listener is unaware, just hearing two lines floating by each other, slightly out of whack, each heading its own direction.

How happy we are

a bit of emphasis and a slide down on "we," as if the very thought were delicious. Then briefly the two rhythms coalesce in satisfaction:

Alone together,
Scholar and cat.

W. H. Auden translated it and Barber turned it into the eighth of his *Hermit Songs*. The voice assumes two characters, the sharp, bold cat and the mild, radiant monk, as each creature goes about his assigned task:

Your shining eye watches the wall;
My feeble eye is fixed on a book.

Triumph comes to each. The voice pounces

You rejoice when your claws entrap a mouse;

Then a smiling, lyric eureka:

I rejoice when my mind fathoms a problem.

The music smoothes out, a kind of boneless feeling, no audible meter. The measures are sometimes in five beats, sometimes in six, as if the bar lines had been casually flung down. A bit of melody in the voice, another bit in the piano, never clear who's going to come in when, the sound of friends interrupting each other, not out of rudeness, but because each gets the point before the other finishes saying it.

> *Pleased with his own art,*
> *Neither hinders the other;*
> *Thus we live ever*
> *Without tedium and envy.*

Key change and we are back to the odd but companionable 1-2-3/1-2 of the beginning. I see them—the cat Pangur perched on a tall cabinet of some sort, looking down on his chosen human. The monk pauses in his studies, feeling feline regard through the top of his tonsured pate. He looks again at what he's written:

> *Pangur, white Pangur,*
> *How happy we are.*

The monk nods at his words and resumes reading. Pangur is still, for the moment, watching.

∞

THE MONK and his cat, so different, and such good friends. In friendship, the easiest thing is to hang out with people like us, but what richness we lose if we cleave only like to like.

A couple of years after the first trip to Aspen, Liz, Sandra, and I were back (Chris had gone to Florida, I think, with the love who was to become her husband). It was while we were hiking one of the Maroon Bells mountains that I began to understand how different we are, in how many realms. We paused for lunch in a lovely Alpine meadow. Liz was tired. Sandra and I wanted to get to the top. Compromise. Liz would relax amid the wildflowers, while Sandra and I fulfilled our need for Gestalt. We would pick up Liz on the descent. A simple thing, recognizing and respecting differences, then working out a solution to give pleasure to all.

My friends let me taste experiences I will never have. They have borne babies. They have lived in foreign countries I will never see. They have built companies. They have scavenged groceries from supermarket dumpsters.

Therein lies wealth. I realized awhile ago that I am only two phone calls away from any help or advice I might need. If I don't know someone, I know someone who knows someone. These people—friends of friends, acquaintances of acquaintances—generously give time and information. I'm no corporate hotshot, no future funding source, but I'm interested in what they're interested in, so they help.

If you're going to be friends with someone who's different than you—ten times richer, can only afford the discount movie, walks with a cane, thinks nothing of running several marathons a year—if you're going to invite that richness into your life—

you're going to have to be generous, creative, respectful, assertive. Generous enough to accept help sometimes. Creative enough to plan events that both of you will enjoy. Respectful of others feelings. And bold enough to point out when the bullshit has reached too high a level.

The days of rehearsals and performances in Aspen are long gone. You can still find Liz and me at rehearsal Monday nights. But Chris is as likely to be in Greece, where she and her husband are renovating the tiny hillside house where his mother was born. Or in Florida. As builders and renovators, they seem to acquire houses the way pet lovers acquire dogs, cats, and fish. Sandra dropped out of the chorus years ago, first to serve on the board of The Saint Paul Chamber Orchestra, and later so she could have the freedom to travel for business and pleasure, now that her kids are up and out.

Liz and I have lunch every week or two. We talk about men and children and rehearsal and use Italian words to discuss music. We plan the recitals that we put on in her living room every eighteen months or so. Then we'll pull out our calendars and choose ten or twelve possible dates, which I'll e-mail to Sandra, who eliminates half because she'll be out of town on business and then e-mails the survivors to Chris, if she's in town. Chris picks a date, and suddenly the four of us are together again.

It takes a bit of effort, maintaining a friendship. Can it be that the friendships formed within the show cast or the reunion committee fell apart after the event because no one bothered to pick up the phone?

When you do make the effort, the reward is grand. Our foursome sparkles. We achieve a kind of balance to the sound: Chris the cello with her low voice and deep reserve—even her problems sound contained; Liz, the laughing flute—always in service to some organization, occasionally even getting paid for it; Sandra, with her smoky saxophone voice, the company boss in her designer suits, free with us to reveal her uncertainties. And me, who knows what my voice sounds like to them?

I like the person I am with them. I'm grateful for the old friends who have seen me at my worst and still choose to be in my life. But more precious still are those in whose presence my worst rarely bothers to show up.

∾

THE DAY we left Aspen, as Liz headed out to the parking lot to pick up the car, I went to Chris and Sandra's room to hurry their packing along. Sandra was propped up on the bed, the phone at her ear, eating yogurt while negotiating a contract. Chris was folding clothes with much precision and tissue paper.

"I dreamt about the four of us last night," I said. "I was going somewhere very important, changing my life, leaving everything behind. They told me I could bring two treasures with me. Just two."

"Which two of us did you pick?" cried Sandra with melodramatic dismay.

"I chose laughter and music. Which is just another name for you guys."

A decade later, I would make the same choice all over again.

Practice for a
Singing Life

*S*o, are you going to practice today?
asks my inner mom.

*Well, sure. But I've got one more phone call to make. The
dishes are dirty. I have to feed the cat.*

I don't hate practicing. I resist it. The goddess of procrastination can seduce me by lifting one eyebrow. After decades of practicing or avoiding same, walking over to the piano remains the hardest part.

Ah. Yes. Here we are again.

Now glissando: a sigh from high to low. Sing nonsense syllables that begin with "nn, mm." Feel the hum. Search for the groove, the buzz, the resonance, the placement, the mask—the one physical space where "AA" flows into "EE" into "AH" into "OH" and the little notes stream easily by—a tone that can travel to the last row of the hall.

The ability to be heard without a microphone determines much of what a classical singer practices: an ability required these days only of opera singers, Shakespearean actors, and pig callers.

Five notes up (do re mi fa sol); five notes down (sol fa mi re do); five times (ee ae ah oh oo). Up a half step. Five notes up, five notes down. The five major vowels. Again.

Scales are an absurd act of faith. Absurd because the human instrument is not articulated that way. *Our* windpipes do not have valves or holes or stops. A singer practicing one scale after another, moving up the keyboard, makes an almost imperceptible muscular adjustment to move the half step from F major to F sharp. To a singer's throat, the number of sharps or flats in each key is irrelevant. A flutist, on the other hand, is keenly aware that F has one flat; F sharp, six sharps. The flutist's fingering for an F sharp major scale is far more complex than the fingering for a major scale in F.

Absurd creatures that singers are, we never question the ritual of singing scales in the same order that instrumentalists practice them, moving up incrementally by half steps.

Scales profess my faith that if I sing enough of these ancient patterns, when the time comes—my mind, my throat, my breath, my tongue will unconsciously coordinate a hundred precise movements so that my spirit can make music.

I once estimated the number of scales I will sing before I die. (Only a singer with an MBA would care to make such a calculation.) In a lifetime of not practicing as much as I should, I will execute a half million or so. The singer in me says, *Fine*. The MBA is puzzled: *Wouldn't you think, after the first ten or twenty thousand, that you'd get it?*

∾

THE GODDESS of procrastination took a vacation while I prepared for my last audition. I actually loved practicing. We audition every year for the Minnesota Chorale. As an independent symphonic chorus, we perform with several orchestras as well as putting on our own concerts. Each performance has its own requirements. A Saint Paul Chamber Orchestra conductor will request a chorus of forty Baroque singers to sing a Bach cantata in German. A Minnesota Orchestra conductor needs one hundred fifty operatic voices to trumpet out the Verdi *Requiem* in Latin. Yet another conductor will request eighty ethereal voices for a Debussy tone poem in French. And then Doc Severinsen, bless him, will ask for one hundred singers who can loosen up and belt out show tunes. Sometimes these performances take place concurrently. Our own chorus conductor makes assignments based on each year's audition. The more flexibility and musicality you demonstrate, the more performances you are offered.

Ninja auditioner, that's me, each year facing the ghostly enemies that undercut my best. First, resentment: The chorus conductor is sitting there judging me! *Get over it, girl. Judging is her job. You go do yours.* Then defensiveness: realizing that I was trying to re-create the very best I'd done in practice, rather than creating music in that moment. *At the audition, your assignment is to find something new in the song. Something you've never noticed before. A breath carried over, a thought that ties the whole thing together. Then take the risk and do it.* Nervous energy channels itself into the search for the music's meaning.

A month before this year's audition: no solos prepared. Up to my ears in choral works, though—soul-rending Old Testament epics. Mendelssohn's *Elijah* had ascended to heaven in a fiery chariot. Kurt Weill's band of long-suffering Jews had built the temple of Solomon in *The Road of Promise*. I was ready for music deeply and profoundly secular.

A tune from Bizet's opera *Carmen* kept wandering through my brain. The gypsy song. Tambourines, seduction—first slow and sizzling, then faster and faster, skirts swirling into a whirlwind, with an orchestra going mad underneath.

Me, Carmen? Well, why not? There are those who might testify to my passion, though I trust they will keep their mouths shut. Still. Plump, old middle-aged me. I loved it.

Found the music buried in the folder labeled ARIAS. Brown and crumbly. Marked 25¢ in pencil. Must have acquired it at some long-ago garage sale. Somebody else's markings scrawled across it. Somebody else's bad translations of the French. Turns and tra la las.

Clean, it has to be clean.

Circling round a note, each pitch distinct and free. And the wildest, fastest singing must be calm underneath. Control and release all swirled together. Delicious. I had to ration my pleasure, especially at the beginning.

Don't sing the whole aria more than once a day. *Well, of course it's fun, but you have to master individual phrases first.* You can't let the storytelling sweep you away before you've implanted the notes in your mind and your muscles. *No, the third time the pattern comes, that interval is a half step, not a whole step. Again.* Got it.

Notice every note, especially when you think you already know the tune. If you get a wrong note into your ear, revising will require you to yank your brain in a painful manner.

Find the most important notes and beats. *Sing just those without any turns or trills. Okay, now add the ornaments.* Turn them

into exercises. Etch half steps and whole steps in crystalline distinc-
tion. No mushy singing. No dwelling in the cracks of the piano.

Clean as a fencer's thrusting foil, almost faster than the ear
can follow, precise movement reveals itself.

*Now the words. Say each one slowly first: Get those vowels
just right. Then recite the poetry until the words flow trippingly
over your American tongue.*

French. My favorite language, with its bittersweet taste in the
mouth. Italian is milk chocolate—vowels all round and smooth,
consonants the briefest excuse to take another bite. German's
consonants are crisp, the vowels bright—a tart apple in the fall.
But French tastes of love and regret with a *soupçon* of bitterness.
Last year's raspberries, pulled from the freezer. They are never
quite as wonderful as that day in the sun when you and your
lover picked them.

I could see the men in the café she was singing to. Feel their
eyes as I gathered my gypsy sisters around me. Hold up my
hands to see rings of brass flashing against brown skin. Feel our
skirts lift in the whirlwind of an ever wilder dance.

"La danse au chant se mariait." Dance and song transport-
ed into a mad fever of a honeymoon.

Two days before audition it wasn't perfect. In the excitement
of it all I would sometimes substitute the words from one verse for
another. But Carmen had infected my blood. I'd listened to the
orchestra on recordings but, due to my sketchy piano skills, I'd
never heard all the notes the piano was supposed to play. This
was my grand opportunity.

I swirled into the audition, a pink and turquoise gauze skirt
hanging from my hips. Explained to the accompanist how the first
verse was to be slow and sultry, then accelerating *"ardentes,*

folles, enfiévrées": ardent, mad, feverish. She informed me that, since she was sight-reading, I probably wasn't going to hear all the piano notes today either. "But" she asked, "can I sing the gypsy girls' part in the tra la's?" Goodness. No audition pianist had ever suggested chiming in before.

"If you can sing that high, sure."

The first ornament was a little hesitant. *No, I will not cower.* The voice clicked into place. Nervous energy channeled itself into spirit, gathering momentum until the final series of tra la la la's, over and over, faster and faster, exploded into laughter—which was mine and Carmen's and the accompanist's.

Haven't received next year's assignments yet. But conductor and accompanist were grinning. They'd been listening to glum art songs all afternoon. If nothing else, we all had a good time, which, presumably, is why we make music.

Practice enables us to play, in every sense of the word. That's the point, which I often forget. On the mirror that I use to correct my mouth position I have taped a note: "If singing were all that serious, frowning would make you sound better."

∾

PRACTICE. To English, by way of French, from the late Latin *practice,* meaning practical. I practice, you practice, he, she, or it practices. Children practice their multiplication tables. But once 12 × 12 is mastered, the word "practice" disappears from school— unless the child takes up an instrument or a sport. It seems odd to me that this fundamental skill of persistence must be acquired extracurricularly.

The military practice maneuvers. Sailors practice man-overboard drills. A doctor practices medicine. And a lawyer?

I wondered whether the practice of music could have anything in common with the practice of law. So I talked to a lawyer
who had started her adult life as a successful professional bas-
soonist. "I worked really, really very hard at the Juilliard," Lynn
told me. (Juilliard teaches students to refer to their school as "*the*
Juilliard." The phrase serves to keep graduates of Oberlin,
Eastman, Curtis, and all the other fine music schools in their
place.) "First of all," continued Lynn, "you go to classes. Then
woodwinds practice probably eight hours a day and you probably
spend four hours making reeds in addition." Serious bassoonists,
oboists, and other woodwind players craft their own reeds—the
pieces of cane that vibrate in their mouthpieces—so the thickness
and flexibility enable the player to produce their best sound with
that particular instrument, in the particular hall they will perform
in. They must shape a reed differently for the humidity of Boston
than for the arid air of Phoenix.

"Then, when your mouth is so tired that you can't play, you
sit and you finger the music through." But when did you sleep?
"You don't much. But if you have a performance at night, you
might not work that hard. You might practice only five hours and
make reeds for two."

The reward for this grueling schedule was a job with the
Orpheus Chamber Orchestra, famous for playing without a con-
ductor, as well as freelance gigs with the New York City Opera, the
Dance Theatre of Harlem, and touring shows that came through
New York. "You get on people's lists," she says, matter-of-factly.
Many musicians would kill for such a life.

Lynn, however, began to feel the joy being sucked out of her
music—by the touring, the control that the chamber orchestra had
over her life, the twenty-four-hour pace of New York. She came

back to Minneapolis/St. Paul, where she freelanced as a musician and worked as a paralegal, eventually deciding to become a lawyer.

After Juilliard, law school came as something of a relief. "I used to practice this many hours a day. Now I was studying this many hours a day. It was great. You didn't have to make reeds and your mouth didn't hurt."

She finds similarities in the analysis that musicians and lawyers must do. "Figuring out the music in the statute. It's not just the notes. It's not just a case. It's the interpretation and how you communicate that interpretation that's going to make all the difference in the world.

"As a musician, you must be detail oriented within this huge framework of the movement or the piece, or how you fit in with the orchestra. That's very true of a lawyer. You have to be very detail oriented, yet make sure you're not drowning the people you're trying to persuade in the mire of details."

And then, of course, there's stage fright. "The same feeling that you have when you play your Carnegie Hall debut—it's the same feeling as walking into a courtroom. The blood drains from my fingers. I get this cotton mouth. But the minute I start to talk, I'm okay. As a musician, I know this feeling and that I'm not going to die."

So lawyers practice interpretation and performing skills for long hours, just like musicians. Yet we don't say a musician *has* a practice—in the sense of a job—the way we do with lawyers and doctors. A family law practice, an internal medicine practice— these imply the application of certain skills over the lifetime of a career. Certainly that's true of many musicians. Why don't I have a choral singing practice? Perhaps because a legal or medical prac- tice has about it an air of stability that hardly applies to a musician's livelihood. After all, a medical practice is an asset that can be bought or sold.

When we make jokes about our doctor practicing oncology and that we hope he's got it right by now, we laugh uneasily. We're uncomfortable, trying to balance ourselves at the intersection of two ideas of practice—doing something over and over to achieve proficiency and a certain kind of job.

At this crossroads, the sacred may dwell. The devout practice a religion, performing its daily rituals. Perhaps we call it practicing because we hope to become a better Jew or Christian or Buddhist or Muslim. But surely we practice a faith because that faith is our living—in the fullest sense of the word——defining much of who we are and how we relate to the world.

Commitment and persistence form the core of practice, every practice.

∽

THE NOTION of practice is conspicuously absent from the halls of corporate America; strange, when you consider the way sports metaphors bounce around the corridors. In over a decade of working with manufacturing, marketing, and training people, I have heard the word in only two contexts: "He was called up before the ethics board for engaging in questionable business practices" and "We want to find out how other companies handle that issue, so we're doing research into 'best practices'" (business speak for what other companies do better than yours). Both uses of "practice" are nouns, not verbs.

Certainly the notion of the typical job in business as a practice in the sense of law or medicine seems absurd. The occupations of accounts payable clerk, manufacturing supervisor, marketing manager, even CEO—none of these have the aura of lifelong vocation with a pool of patients or clients to whom the owner of the practice is accountable.

I have this fantasy of a CEO making a presentation to his company. The big auditorium is filled with the whole range of employees—from exec VPs to cafeteria workers. Audiovisual technicians are scrambling about, broadcasting the presentation through the MegaCompany Global Television Network to New York, Beijing, London, Dubuque. As the CEO speaks, a huge TV screen fills with razzle-dazzle, computer-generated graphics—bar charts, happy customers, pie charts, pretty products, lists of noble aspirations (the words set off by tidy bullet points). He reaches the upbeat climax that impressed stockholders at the annual meeting the day before. Then he pauses, turns the computer graphics off. The place gets quiet and dark. All you see now is this one, human guy, up there on stage with a microphone. He says, "It's all true, all those great numbers, and our goals. But it's not the whole truth. There's a mistake we as a company tend to make over and over. We're good at working around it, and accomplishing what we want in spite of it. But I'm tired of it. I think we can do better. I think we can change rather than compensate. But that means we need to practice—individually and as an organization. We know what to do—we've studied other companies who can do this. We just need the courage to persistently practice something we're going to be lousy at, at first.

"And to make it safe for all of us to experiment and try new ways of practicing this skill, I'm going to suspend layoffs for two years."

Ah, well, a person can dream. Practice flourishes in a space that is safe enough for honesty, that allows mistakes. A place where you can risk failure because you know you'll be there to practice again tomorrow.

∽

BY PRACTICING we seek to achieve *reliable* excellence—in sickness and health, for better for worse. Such a simple idea. But under the stress of performance, even Olympic figure skaters trip over moves they've executed perfectly hundreds of times in practice.

Which makes Payne Stewart's performance on the 18th hole of the 1999 U.S. Open all the more extraordinary. An uphill putt of fifteen feet. One stroke would win him the title. Two strokes would tie the game and take him to a sudden death match the next day. The commentator said "unlikely under this kind of pressure." The crowd was cheering as he walked to the ball. He frowned slightly, looking neither right nor left. As if he was not allowing into his mind applause or winning or prize money, but only the task at hand. Silence. Carefully, methodically, Stewart took a couple of practice swings, then hit the ball. It rolled gently up the hill, traversed the final plateau, then just as gently sank into the cup. Pandemonium. He leaped into the air, fist shooting up in triumph. Swooped his caddie off the man's feet. Nearly kissed him. Then did kiss his wife.

He was forty-two. That's old to be at the top of his golf game, they kept saying. But it seems to me that age gives us the opportunity to acquire a practice *of* practice. To come to know the foibles of the unique creature we bring to our practice. To acquire a bag of practical tricks that get the desired result out of this performer. To practice analyzing the results of our performance: what worked, what didn't. What will I do the same next time, what differently? Then to use that information the next time, and learn from that experience.

∽

I HAVE practiced hope. *Help me to feel every drop of love and of joy that are here on this Earth for me today.* I started saying that years ago, after my last bout of depression. Not asking for the world to change, not always clear who I'm asking. But every day, clearly asking. The day begins. I forget about it. But I notice life differently than I used to.

∽

"HOW DID I get to be so *old*?" my mother asked, when she turned seventy-five.

"By getting out of bed every morning," I told her.

∽

PRACTICE builds the foundation—that which everything else rests on, unseen, essential. When we practice, we not only acquire skill, but we become a different kind of instrument: humble, because we've seen our performance at its worst, but also patient, persistent, demanding, and determined.

It doesn't matter much *what* we practice. It matters very much *that* we practice.

∽

WHEN TODAY'S scales are sung, notes learned, phrases polished, fears faced, I close the keyboard. I turn on the phone, admit distraction. But the focused vibration so carefully cultivated hums through my body the rest of the day.

Conductor
Watching

We prepare for the coming of Robert Shaw as if he were an emperor. By the second rehearsal I'm figuring he'd better be wearing one hell of an outfit.

Anticipation verging on fear vibrates in the rehearsal room. It's not just the fourteen Grammies, the Kennedy Center Honors. It's the soprano who shows up with a treasured book containing blurry photocopies of purple mimeographs (the copying technology that prevailed in the ancient days before Xerox): "My mother sang with Shaw in the Cleveland Symphony Orchestra Chorus back in the sixties. She kept his notes." Kathy Saltzman Romey, our chorus conductor, tells us that her father's studies with Shaw were interrupted when he got the word that his wife was in labor, birthing Kathy. Now, forty-some-odd years later, Kathy will lead the first eight rehearsals before Shaw joins us.

Shaw was preparing choruses to sing under Arturo

Toscanini's baton in 1945, six years before I was born. He is one of the few choral conductors to cross over to the position of orchestral conductor, first as an associate conductor of the Cleveland Orchestra under George Szell, then for twenty-one years as music director of the Atlanta Symphony Orchestra. Shaw is nearly eighty. This may be my only chance to sing with him.

What does a piece of history look like? Can it take a joke?

Robert Shaw will be conducting us and the Minnesota Orchestra in an evening centered around the medieval poem *"Stabat Mater Doloroso"* ("Sorrowfully the mother stood"). We will begin with the men singing the original Gregorian chant, then sing settings of the poems by three composers. The three versions were first performed between 1898 and 1950. They could not be more different.

Giuseppe Verdi wrote a Verdi opera, bless him. Twelve minutes long, with one character—the chorus—but still, the story of Mary's mourning Christ and the narrator's hope for salvation are rendered in the eminently singable tradition of Italian opera.

I'm grateful that Francis Poulenc's version scatters rays of sunlight throughout the dark grief, but the man seems to believe that chords should be constructed of notes layered on top of one another like the dough in baklava. When you have seven different notes in a chord instead of the conventional three or four, you'd better sing perfectly in tune: The effect is either shimmering beauty or an ugly mess.

And then there is Karol Szymanowski (pronounced "shiman-AHV-ski"), the least well known of the composers. In 1926 he was commissioned to write a Polish requiem. He filled his harmonies with lush, fierce mother love. Polish mother love. He had the Latin poem translated into his mother tongue, and that, gang, is how we are going to sing it.

As we work our way through the eight rehearsals allocated to prepare before Shaw arrives, "Oh, boy" gradually fizzles into "Oh, no." We find ourselves spending hour after hour not singing, but copying Shaw's notations into our scores. A chorus wants to know as much about the orchestra conductor's interpretation as possible. We are pleased to pencil in tempos, phrasing, breath marks, and so forth before we actually join the orchestra conductor for the final three rehearsals. But Shaw expects us to draw something over every single note. One typical measure: Place the appropriate combination of lines and dots to indicate the four notes in the bar as, respectively, *legato, tenuto, portato,* and *staccato*; draw a phrase mark over the whole; add a comma for the breath and a line to indicate where to place the final consonant. Then on to the next measure.

When we're not scribbling on the music, we're learning to pronounce Polish. Karol Szymanowski believed that by setting his *Stabat Mater* in the vernacular, he would portray Mary's universal *human* suffering. A fine aspiration, but tough on an American chorus. We have sung in English, German, French, Spanish, Italian, Hebrew, Russian, as well as three pronunciations of Latin, but never have I struggled as I did with Polish. Our Polish-language coach Iwona (pronounced "ee-VON-ah") said each word slowly, then wrinkled her forehead in concentration listening to us strive to imitate her. So many consonants; and the vowels, so different from English—especially the nasal glide, a kind of human *meow* that comes at the end of some words.

A small victory—the rich taste of the word for "cross." We see *krzyza* and say "KSHIH-zhah." Iwona's forehead smoothes and the wrinkles reappear at the corners of her eyes, punctuating her smile. "Yes, that's it."

The difficulty with Polish isn't Shaw's fault, other than his choosing this piece. But the mathematical mind-set is definitely his. Kathy announces that each of the four sections—soprano, alto, tenor, bass—will be divided yet again into six subsections. Each subsection may be assigned to sing a few notes from another part at any time. My score fills with little arrows sending me up to the soprano part and down to the tenor at odd moments. If the composer wanted it sung like that, why didn't he just write it that way? Who is Shaw to be correcting Verdi?

Finally, we get to sing—sort of. Forget the words for now, we're singing "ONE-ee-and-a-TWO-ee-and-a-THREE-ee-and-a-FOUR-ee-and-a": syllables that tell us exactly which fraction of the beat each pitch is on.

Kathy never seems to exhale during the long hours of trying to get us to get it right. Her conducting becomes stiffer, her smiles tight lipped and nervous. Her stress infects us, compounding our frustration.

Barb Brooks, our accompanist, advises me to have patience: "What separates Shaw from other choral conductors is his sense of inner pulse and rhythm, the blood that makes the music come alive."

Shaw's notes to his Cleveland chorus reflected this passion: "Little notes are just as important as big notes," Shaw told them. "Sixteenths and eighths and quarters are not just things that come between bigger things . . . I get a horrible picture from the way you sing, of little bitty eighth notes running like hell all over the place to keep from being stepped on . . . Look, this is a democracy . . . Eighth notes can vote."

We trudge on, mastering markings and mechanics. I conclude that Shaw is either (a) a compulsive control freak, who doesn't trust singers to be able to take direction or (b) a visual learner who believes that writing all this down will imprint it in our brains.

It turns out neither interpretation captured it all.

∽

FINALLY, the big night arrives—first piano rehearsal with Shaw at Orchestra Hall. The stage looks barren without the orchestra—just a podium for the conductor, a piano, and risers and chairs for the chorus. The tenor beside me worries: "What if he walks in, takes a listen and announces 'They don't know the music' and storms out, never to work with us again? I heard of a conductor who did that."

"Was it Shaw?" I ask.

"I don't think so, but still."

Shaw enters while Kathy is warming us up. He waves a hand—indicating she should continue—takes a seat and listens. We call upon our peripheral vision, keeping half an eye on her and most of our attention on him. Big guy. Kind, open face.

Warm-up complete, Kathy begins, "It is my honor to intro-duce one of the great conductors—"

"Yah, yah, yah," Shaw interrupts, brushing off the accolades with a flick of his wrist. We laugh. He's human.

He asks Kathy to conduct the Verdi, and again takes his seat to listen. Kathy's tension over the past two months has made her conducting gestures fierce and rigid, trapped inside an invisible box in front of her body. But now some spirit moves her, some transformation. Her arms open from the heart, like a dancer's. Her whole body flows, and our voices bloom into music.

We're ready. A collective exhalation rejoices the air after the last note.

∞

SHAW TAKES us through some of his exercises, and they come alive: We sing an F, as softly as possible, on "oo."

"No, listen. Tune it. Good. Now crescendo and open to 'ah.' "

A C shimmers above our unison F. Magic: a note sounding without being sung.

"Again. Keep the fifth in the room."

And again the C—a fifth above the note we're singing—materializes, clear and strong, with the pure sound of a boys' choir.

Every music theory student learns that each note has within it many other notes—a series of overtones. A clarinet emphasizes different overtones than a violin, which is why the two instruments sound different even when playing the same pitch. But this overtone is no theoretical construct. It is a vibrating fact created by 185 voices singing exactly the same note.

"You can increase the size of your chorus," Shaw says, "with overtones. Just by singing in tune. Then no orchestra in the world can overpower you." Practical advice from a man who has been making sure the audience can hear the chorus for longer than I've been alive.

He explains his dedication to all those lines and dots we've been drawing: "All the factors of music are factors of the spirit." He believes this. For Shaw, intonation and rhythm are acts of homage. Precision forges a collection of singers into a single instrument that exalts the individual: "Choral music is the only unity of humanity that doesn't involve betrayal of the self. It only ennobles each one of us."

He tells stories about the composers. "Do you realize that when Verdi died, fifty thousand people followed his casket through the streets? Like he was one of the Beatles." Shaw describes the holy water in the chapel Poulenc attended, and the acoustics. Shaw went there to learn, to understand: "The place has been holy for probably thirty-five hundred years," sacred long before Christianity. This pagan spirituality underlies the bittersweet lightness of Poulenc's *Stabat Mater*. What we comprehend, we can convey. Like children listening to bedtime stories, we are completely absorbed. We see worlds beyond our knowing.

Best of all, he has such fun on the podium. His foot slaps the floor: one-AND-two-AND. . . . His eyes twinkle; his elbows lift. He looks like a delighted chicken. He turns his head to the side, eyes closed, listening to a long phrase. Then he stops us and smears a big smack of an air kiss across the entire chorus.

But it's his hands I want a picture of. Long, pianist's fingers, cupping the notes in the air, beckoning the music. Sometimes the left hand imitates the baton position of the right—thumb and forefinger together—as he gestures for more precision.

A chorus can be seduced by the beauty of a conductor's hands.

∞

WEDNESDAY MORNING, we troop on stage for dress rehearsal with orchestra before that night's performance. Chairs, music stands are all in place. But where are the instrumentalists? Kathy announces, tears in her eyes, "Mr. Shaw woke up with chest pains. He gave me his notes, then left to see a doctor and go back to his hotel to rest. You know where to place your prayers."

Kathy spends the next two hours working through Shaw's

notes on the difficult spots. The stage is full of sound, but feels empty. "What'll we do if he can't go on tonight?" we ask each other. We'll be back in seven hours. Then we'll know.

A somber afternoon to reflect on this man and what it is he does.

∞

WHO AM I to talk about what makes a conductor great?

Critics and scholars have written reams on conducting. They sit in the tenth row, orchestra center, and judge who brings the music alive, who draws gorgeous sound and fine musicianship from a hundred players who have played Beethoven's Fifth times beyond remembering.

I don't hear what they hear. I sit in the second row of the alto section, where the sound leans heavily toward altos, tenors, and French horns. (The only thing I miss about singing soprano is sitting stage right and watching the show the percussionists put on—bells, ratchets, cymbals, gongs, timpani. Now I've moved left, toward center stage, overlooking brass and woodwinds. The most entertainment the French horns offer is squinting at the copies of *Car and Driver* that sit on their music stands to occupy them while they're counting 243 bars of rest.)

I can't speak to the myriad of other tasks performed by the conductor who is also the orchestra's music director—choosing repertoire, designing programs, stroking donors, attracting new audiences. My musical life is focused on the small proportion of concerts that include choral music.

But I can do this with confidence: I can tell you who drew something extraordinary out of me and those around me, who revealed the music and expressed it clearly and powerfully, who unified and inspired. And I can report what was happening at the time.

I believe this has validity. Because when those who are playing or singing are inspired, it frequently carries to the tenth row and beyond.

Why does great conducting matter to those of us who don't aspire to the job? Obviously, if we know who the great conductors are, we can attend their concerts, buy their recordings. But far more than that, conducting is visible leadership. Those who wish to lead in business, politics, at home, can learn from a conductor's techniques and qualities. But even those of us who prefer to be off working by ourselves still get stuck leading from time to time. Perhaps we have kids—or acquire them temporarily—and we're trying to get them to work together on a project. Or we find ourselves in a business meeting where we happen to know more about the subject at hand than anyone else in the room and our expertise plops us into leadership. Or we care so deeply, so passionately about some issue that suddenly we find everyone is listening to our ideas and expecting us to tell them what to do. For those times when we achieve the leadership we desire or accept the reality that we are already playing that role, it behooves us to notice what works from the podium. It pays to watch the conductor.

What, in fact, is conducting? Back in 1752, Johann Joachim Quantz, in his essay "Method for Playing the Transverse Flute," wrote that "a good leader . . . must know how to introduce reasonable and proper discipline. If his services have earned him respect, and his friendly demeanour and affable conduct have brought him affection, this will not be difficult." By 1965 this gentle aspect had shifted considerably. *The Oxford Companion to Music* begins its entry on the subject: "Conducting is generalship on the battlefield of music." The author goes on to explain that he is referring to the large and small forces that must be controlled by the conductor. But who, I wonder, is the enemy? This military image pervades Elliott W. Galkin's descriptions of some of the great conductors of the twentieth century in *A History of Orchestral Conducting in Theory and Practice*: "On the podium, Koussevitzky was unmistakably the personification of authority, presiding over his orchestra like a battalion commander." Von Karajan, Galkin says, "paces his way to the podium with deliberate imperiousness, as if a military leader about to inspect his troops."

But then we come upon Simone Young, in an interview with the *New York Times,* before her 1996 debut conducting at the Metropolitan Opera: "When people talk about conducting—the maestro myth—they talk about power. Conducting has nothing to do with power. It has everything to do with forgetting your personal self, immersing yourself in this music, making the music speak to the audience and doing that together with the forces you are working with. But what the public sees is somebody waving their arms around and everybody following." And Bobby McFerrin, who talked with me before conducting his first Fauré *Requiem* with the Saint Paul Chamber Orchestra and the Minnesota Chorale (also in 1996): "The kind of conducting that I want to achieve in my life, and I'm probably many, many years away from that, is almost like Zen conducting, where you have your ideas, but you also get your ideas from others. Because I don't think anyone can know everything by themselves. Then you make music together. The conductor can get out of the way, become a guardian, rather than a traffic cop."

∾

WE ARE fascinated by the person up there waving the stick. Audience, musicians, critics, musicologists—we watch and analyze. We vilify and deify, turning conductors into stars. Oh, the accoutrements of stardom may change over the years. Serge Koussevitzky, who served as music director of the Boston Symphony Orchestra from 1924 to 1949, wore a crimson-lined velvet cape and was reputed to own ninety pairs of shoes. Fast-forward to the 1990s. Bobby McFerrin, in his early days of conducting the Saint Paul Chamber Orchestra, walks on stage wearing a black silk shirt, no tie. He sits down, takes his shoes off, and suggests that the orchestra do so, too.

But whatever sartorial statement they make, conductors receive our prayer: "Make magic for us. Reveal the music. Do something to the sound that we have never heard before, that pierces body and soul."

We didn't always ask so much. The leader of a medieval church choir moved his or her right hand up and down to remind singers of their notes. This conductor held a staff in the left hand, a symbol of the office. When free-flowing Gregorian chant metamorphosed into melodies with a specific number of beats per measure, the leader indicated the first beat by moving the staff down and the second beat by gesturing up. (In triple meter, the gesture was down for beats one and two, and up for beat three.) Thus the down beat and up beat were born.

In 1687, the staff was still in use, and using it proved suicidal to French composer and conductor Lully. As was customary in those days, he conducted by hitting the staff against the floor, audibly beating time to keep everyone together (a practice that continued to annoy music lovers for many generations: Rousseau complained about it in his *Dictionary of Music* nearly a century later). Lully missed the floor and hit his own foot, which developed an abscess and then gangrene, from which he died.

We still consider conducting a dangerous profession. The pressure, the spotlight—they add to our fascination with this gladiator who must dance on edge of triumph or catastrophe for the length of a two-hour concert. Yet in 1980 the Metropolitan Life Insurance Company published findings from a twenty-year study of 437 symphony orchestra and opera conductors. The report concluded, "Men who direct the symphony orchestras of the nation do indeed enjoy superior longevity."

But then these days, conductors have abandoned the staff and taken up the baton.

∾

THE MUSIC reference books—*The Grove Dictionary*, *The Oxford Companion*—are fixated on that baton—how it developed, who used it, who didn't, and why—as if the symbol of the office were the act itself. The baton has taken on the aura of a magician's wand; yet the maestro standing on the podium waving a baton is a fairly recent phenomenon. The practice solidified only in the mid-nineteenth century. Public concerts haven't been around all that long either. The first public concert on record in England was in 1672—thirteen years before Bach and Handel were born, but it was only in the nineteenth century that "public concerts begin to achieve a mass following . . . when the Industrial Revolution produced an affluent merchant class devoted to amusement, self-improvement, and recreational social climbing," according to Robert Jourdain, author of *Music, the Brain, and Ecstasy.* Prior to these public concerts of the nineteenth century, common people listened to sophisticated music primarily in church. Rich people kept private orchestras as status symbols like jewels or furnishings.

The first violinist in such a private orchestra would frequently set the tempo by waving his bow. (Perhaps in deference to this role, Americans and Germans refer to the first violinist as "concertmaster," while the British refer to him or her as the "leader.")

Alternatively—especially if vocal music was involved—the conductor might direct from the harpsichord, where he would also play continuo and accompany the singers. In the mid-eighteenth century, C. P. E. Bach held that this was the best method for instrumental music as well.

In eighteenth-century opera, there were often *two* conductors: the first violinist led the orchestra, and a second conductor, seated at the keyboard, was responsible for the singers—soloists and chorus. This bizarre system, with its inherent invitation to conflict, persisted well into the next century. In 1847 when Mendelssohn conducted the first London performance of his oratorio *Elijah* (with a baton), the *Times* critic complained, "Mr. Perry, the leader, was constantly beating time with his fiddlestick in such a manner as to obstruct the view of the conductor and to confuse the attention of the instrumentalists."

By the civilized twentieth century, the battle of the dueling conductors was long over. A sole conductor stood firmly established as the orchestral focal point. One would think peace would reign. One would be wrong. Throughout a career that stretched from the last few years of the nineteenth century well into the mid-twentieth, Arturo Toscanini raged at singers and instrumentalists alike. He snapped batons between his hands. He was not unique. Fritz Reiner's tenure at the Pittsburgh Symphony Orchestra from 1938 to 1948 was known as his "reign of terror." One year the attrition rate for musicians was 45 percent (retired, fired, or left for other orchestras). Perhaps to compensate for his large temper, Reiner kept time with small, almost imperceptible gestures. The most famous Pittsburgh musician to get the ax was a string bassist who whipped out a long spyglass during a concert, focusing it on Reiner's tiny beat. He earned not only unemployment but also a place in history as a folk hero to orchestra musicians everywhere.

A conductor's temper can leave scars, even when the musicians understand the maestro's frustration. Fred Zimmerman experienced Toscanini's outbursts as a string bass player with the NBC Symphony Orchestra. Frequently Toscanini knew exactly what he wanted and assumed the musicians would—or should— know, too. When they didn't, Toscanini became inarticulate and furious. One time, Zimmerman says, Toscanini "glared at the basses and said: 'You are stupid, eh? You are stupid? Answer me!'; and we nodded our heads. 'You are jackasses? Answer me!'; and we nodded our heads again. Many embarrassing and painful minutes were wasted, instead of the correction that could have been made immediately." Another time there was an accent on a note in a passage of Smetana's *Bartered Bride* that none of the musicians had noticed or played before. Toscanini made them play it over and over. As Zimmerman tells it, after several playings, Toscanini "said 'Is not accent on this note?' And he stormed at us for not noticing the accent ourselves. That was thirty years ago: and every time I play those two bars I have a trauma—I hear the Old Man shouting."

A conductor can't throw things at the orchestra these days. The unions won't allow it. The balance of power has shifted. Some orchestras—Vienna, Berlin, and the Royal Concertgebouw in Amsterdam—are actually managed by the musicians. In

America, when a new music director is needed, musicians from the orchestra typically work with the Board of Trustees in the selection process.

∞

So, IF CONDUCTORS can't rule by fear anymore, what can they do? What did Shaw do that was so special?

Shaw, more than any conductor I've worked with before or since, literally embodied the essential dynamic of precision and passion—the yin/yang—that lies at the heart of music making. A fancy way of speaking. I asked my friend Liz what she loved best about Shaw. Without pausing a beat, she said "His elbows. I could get everything I needed just by watching his elbows." The beat, the attitude, the phrasing, even the glory—every morsel of his body manifested the music. We probably could have seen the music in his kneecaps if he'd been wearing shorts.

For Shaw there was no conflict between precision and passion. At first I tolerated all those meticulous exercises because I thought, *All right, we're developing a honed instrument for Shaw to play upon. We'll get it right first so we can get to the music.* But for Shaw, I realized, holding that eighth note its full value *is* making music. That tiny eighth note has individual significance to the whole piece. Just as one lone alto among 45 altos, among 185 singers, among the several hundred musicians on stage— that one alto has significance as well.

He had no idea who I was. Yet I knew I was important to him, not personally, but to the moments of music, the totality of experience we were creating.

This sense of individual importance cannot be taken for granted. Instrumentalists in the last row of a section have been known to say "I could phone in my performance, for all the difference it makes." Possibly true for violinists (though I doubt it). Definitely untrue for singers. During one typically overworked summer festival, guest conductor Christopher Seaman looked at the earnest, exhausted chorus he had been given. Too many works to prepare in too few rehearsals. And the piece before him was Carl Orff's *Carmina Burana*—which needs to be loud, pagan, tender, soft—each mood outrageously itself. Seaman stopped conducting. His red hair remained standing on end from exertion. His pale British face grew calm, his voice dry. "This piece is meant to be fun. Please notify your faces." Laughter. Suddenly, every singer was engaged. So were our smile muscles. Tighten those, and you change the shape of the vowels, which changes the quality of the sound dramatically.

A singer who is engaged will do a thousand things right, too many to think about in the moment, too many for any conductor to mention in the short minutes of rehearsal.

Humor engages, far more effectively than terror. I treasure a moment of Kathy Romey's conducting, preparing us for that same *Carmina Burana*. She stood before us, her usually slim figure large with pregnancy, at a loss: how to get us to be heard at the end of the first movement. Mere volume would never carry our sound over the full fortissimo of the strings, brass, and woodwinds in front of us. "I need more. Focus. A laser beam," her voice rose in crescendo. "I want to feel *fetal movement*!" She got it. No one but Kathy in that moment could have made that remark. Ridiculous and effective.

The funny moments are etched in my brain, clear as the moments of terror for Toscanini's musicians. Bobby McFerrin was rehearsing us for a concert performance of Gershwin's *Porgy and*

Bess. He had such a mixed bag of a chorus to work with—the mostly white Minnesota Chorale, which performs classical music; the half white/half black Leigh Morris Chorale, which sings African-American spirituals, gospel, and jazz; and the mostly black members of several of gospel church choirs. Singing Gershwin well meant the classically trained Midwesterners had to loosen up, a difficult task for many. Trying harder doesn't always work, no matter what German and Scandinavian emigrants taught their children. Bobby was experimenting with one idea after another.

Then a voice came from the soprano section, "Bobby . . . ?" Bit of an uplift at the end of the word, not exactly a question, not exactly a demand.

"Yes, Mom?"

It was, in fact, Bobby's mom, Sara Copper McFerrin, retired chair of the Fullerton College Music Department. She had sung in the chorus of the movie of *Porgy and Bess* in 1959. Now, nearly forty years later, she had flown in from California to sing with us. (A McFerrin family affair, that movie. The voice you hear in the movie when Sidney Poitier sings "Bess, you is my woman now," is that of Bobby's dad, opera singer Robert McFerrin.)

"Yes, Mom?" Bobby's eyebrows moved up, wrinkling his forehead. He flashed a self-conscious grin at us. Suddenly, this was not Bobby McFerrin, famous-jazz-vocalist-turned-conductor. This was little Bobby, waiting for Mom to lay down the law.

"This section is supposed to be gossipy. We're gossiping to one another."

He looked at us and shrugged: "You heard Mom."

We sang it that way. It worked.

The humor that turns a chorus into music itself has a quality

I call "thisness." No canned jokes, but the peculiar, particular statements that emerge at this moment in time, with this chorus, this orchestra, this piece, this conductor. The humor that emerges from a human being who is being completely him- or herself at that moment. Kathy the bossy woman and joyful mother-to-be. Bobby the big star and little boy. Shaw, who sees the divine vista from the mountaintop, and notices when one lousy eighth note is too short or too long. Whatever alchemist composed human beings mixed in a lot of contradictory elements. Humor enables us to live them all richly and concurrently, and to put any combustion to good, musical use.

I am especially grateful when a conductor makes me laugh, because classical choral music, for all that I love it, is rarely funny. When humor appears in the choral literature (as it does in *Carmina Burana*), it tends to be masculine: the guys get the drinking songs and the women get to be angelic.

Christopher Seaman told me, "You can't really teach conducting, although you can learn it." He says this as one who trains young conductors at the Guildhall School for Music & Drama in London, in addition to conducting various orchestras around the world. "There are certain basics. You have to be clear. Otherwise the orchestra gets confused. And you can't expect people to play quietly if you're thrashing about. But apart from that, somehow people have to be themselves, to get into a voyage of self-discovery and find out what gets the best out of others."

Conductors—and all leaders—can learn through observation—not in order to imitate, but to see the universe of possibilities that are available to them. When Seaman finished his studies at King's College, Cambridge, he did what any young, ambitious conductor might do: He got himself a job playing timpani with the

London Philharmonic. He figured that since the timpanist doesn't play very often, he'd have lots of time for conductor watching.

Each conductor brings a particular bundle of attributes—personality, musical knowledge, their own experience playing an instrument or singing—to a particular situation. Odd that each situation is unique. This orchestra and chorus may have performed Beethoven's Ninth together twenty-five times in the last decade, perhaps even with this conductor. But still, this orchestra and this chorus does not necessarily mean these same instrumentalists, these same singers. Even given the same personnel, everyone's life has changed since the last performance, and the world, too. Beethoven's Ninth will never be the same to those who saw Bernstein conducting it over the rubble of the fallen Berlin Wall.

∾

THISNESS lies at the heart of things, the heart not only of humor, but of power. Great leaders know their internal resources—who they are and what they have to give—as well as their external resources—what is available in this time, this place, with this orchestra and chorus, for this audience. They gather the forces of thisness together, beckoning with that magic wand of a baton, and conjure music. They welcome power, open to it, channel it, and allow it to reign.

The great leaders are conduits of power, which is very hard work. Conductors sweat a lot.

Ultimately conducting *is* about power, despite how some younger conductors talk. It has to be, or the audience is left unmoved. But the power is not despotic and never really has been. Nor is it a matter of the trappings of office. We see a conductor's velvet cape, a business executive's fancy office. These are only props, sets, costumes: They are not the energy that changes reality—which is what happens when great leadership is present. The trappings do not necessarily even indicate the presence of such energy.

Power is the accomplishment of intentions. Simply that. A leader is someone who accomplishes those intentions through and with others. The true leader in that conference room may be the quiet person in the corner taking notes.

A seven-figure salary, an office so big you could safely send a bowling ball on its way to a strike—don't confuse these with power. Or a boss with a leader.

"My girls don't clean unless there's hot water," declared the woman in her flat, Maine accent. She supervised the chambermaids in the resort I worked at one summer during college. She said it to her boss—a fat, sleazy fellow who saved money by not turning on the water heater till the day before the guests arrived He had also disconnected the odometer of the Lincoln Continental he rented from his brother-in-law.

That one sentence spoke eloquently: We were *her* girls—important persons, worthy of proper tools. Cleaning those cabins after a long Maine winter was important work, worth doing properly. She had pride in her work, in herself, and in us, and no cheapskate boss was going to deter her from doing good work well.

The boss turned on the hot water, we cleaned, and the staff got hot showers. Who had the power here? He drove a Lincoln, she drove an old beater. But who was a leader? Sure, he wanted clean cabins, too. But when the labor market gets tight, who is sure to attract employees?

Her girls didn't clean with cold water. Indeed not. Or forget to dust under the bed, or omit to wash the floor behind the toilet. Her spot checks kept us meticulous and proud. If someone can instill such pride in a group of college students, most of whose parents had "help" at home doing these same tasks, think what we should be able to do with tasks that are inherently grand.

I think of that stalwart Maine lady, and I think of Robert Shaw—of hot water properly applied and eighth notes given their full value. They understood complete dedication to the job at hand.

∾

SHAW WAS an evangelist. He came from a family of evangelical preachers and meant to be a minister himself. In college, he majored in religion and philosophy. But directing the college glee club led to a job with Fred Waring, the popular radio band leader, organizing and leading the Fred Waring Glee Club. Then, frustrated at conducting only pop music, Shaw formed the Collegiate Chorale. This led to a gig with Toscanini and the NBC Symphony Orchestra, which led him to form the Robert Shaw Chorale, which led him to Cleveland, then Atlanta and the rest of his illustrious career. But he never stopped preaching. The doctrine was the glory of the human spirit expressed through music.

Like all spiritual disciplines, it demanded everything—from himself, from those who chose to work with him. He mastered the art of always demanding more, while instilling in his followers the belief that they were absolutely capable of what he was demanding.

Musicians continued to play under Toscanini, in spite of his abuse, because, as one said, "however well you played, with him you found yourself playing better."

"I am larger, better than I thought," Walt Whitman says in

Song of the Open Road, "I did not know I held so much goodness." That's what it felt like to sing under Shaw.

Excellence makes us feel like gods, all the more powerful
because we serve something larger than ourselves. The great conductors take us to Olympus. Their methods may vary—a clear
beat, evangelical preaching, temper tantrums, the ability to make
stressed musicians laugh—but they take us to some place golden
and fine that we might not otherwise find on our own. To guide
us there, they must know the geography of the place. The composer provides the map. Then the conductor must go there in
imagination: note the sound of water rushing over a single peb-
ble in a stream, struggle to the top of the highest hill, embrace the
vista. Finally, gathering all the resources of his or her particular
combination of body, mind, and spirit, the conductor must manifest this vision so clearly that followers can see the landscape
before them, so powerfully that followers flame with desire to
bring music into this world.

∾

WE LEAVE Orchestra Hall at noon after what was supposed to have
been dress rehearsal for the *Stabat Mater* concerts, each singer
wondering if Shaw would conduct us for our first performance
that night. We move through our afternoon tasks for job and family, uneasy, half present. *No phone call canceling the performance. That's a good sign, but hardly conclusive.* We eat dinner,
don black dress or tux, head back downtown through rush-hour
traffic, walk through the stage door and into the hall to warm up.
We hope.

Kathy's smile seems larger than her face. "Mr. Shaw will be

joining us in a few minutes." *Thank God*. The thought, magnified in the minds of 185 sopranos, altos, tenors, and basses, is nearly audible. There's a feeling of 185 stretched rubber bands relaxing. Murmurs go round, spreading rumors and theories: "I hear it was something he ate."

"Well, you know how indigestion can seem like a heart attack."

"Hallelujah," murmurs the worried tenor next to me. "I thought we were going to go down in history as the chorus that killed Robert Shaw."

(Shaw continued to conduct nearly until his death in 1999. No chorus, thank heavens, had to take on that designation.)

That March night, music's grievous loss still three years away, Shaw makes his entrance. Pale and a bit tentative, the old trouper is *there*.

"The last few days, I feel like I've been stamped 'Return to sender,' " he tells us, "but you have great doctors in this town." He warms us up, slowly, softly, as is his custom: He rarely allows singers to sing loudly in rehearsal. Then the preacher sermonizes on how important each of us is, and how important our job: "Every time you do a concert like this, you're placing a vote for the human spirit."

As he exits, we stand and cheer. "Oh, well," he says, "there goes my warm-up."

∽

A FEW minutes later, on stage, in front of an audience, we discover what we lost because Shaw was too ill to conduct the final rehearsal. The sound of a hundred women thinking—*He didn't cue us; I must have counted wrong*—is very quiet. By the time we realize we did count right, the entrance is long gone, replaced by a bar and a half of silence.

The next day Shaw promises Kathy, "I'll cue them, darling, I'll cue them." And for the second performance, he does—a bar early—but by that time, nothing on earth could have prevented our nailing that entrance. Each night's performance goes better than the last, as Shaw regains his physical confidence and joy.

∽

DURING THE last intermission, I introduce myself to Shaw. Normally, I wouldn't have had the chutzpah, but I am briefly *persona* extremely *grata* among the Chorale. An article I've written about him and these performances has appeared in the *St. Paul Pioneer Press,* one of the two major newspapers in town. (Very big deal, since Twin Cities critics often ignore choruses to the point of pathology. How can a critic review *Messiah* and not mention the chorus till the penultimate paragraph?) I tell him I'm the author of the newspaper piece. He looks blank for a minute. Then says, "Thank you for writing the article, but I never read that stuff. My secretary, Miss Frink, is collecting all the articles in a book, and I'm going to read it when I'm dead."

I can't imagine he has the time. I'm sure he's much too busy getting the heavenly host to sing in tune so we can hear their overtones.

Balm in Gilead

*I*t is fall, gray, damp. I want so much—not to die, exactly, but to stop the hurting. I keep my body moving. Left foot, right, left foot, right. I can do this. The asphalt path inert below, the Mississippi sluggish in the distance. My face is marked by two wet streaks, but I am *not* crying. One does not cry in public. It's bad manners. In poor taste. Unless, of course, you're on stage and the part calls for it. But even then, you don't really cry before you sing, because you won't be able to sing. Or so my mother taught me.

I want so much to slit my wrists and watch the red blood flow far away. I cannot breathe. There is no life in the air.

Sometimes

It is my own mouth moving. The thread of a sound, down in the low notes I can still make after I've been crying and the vocal cords are swollen.

I feel

Short phrases that require no air at all

Like a motherless child

The line pulls me

Sometimes
I feel like a motherless child

Then higher, stronger, the pain more naked and pure

Sometimes I feel like a motherless child
A long way

I follow "way" as it dips low, mourning the immense distance

From home

The "oh" of home stretches, moans from somewhere deep in my gut, and I affirm sadly

a long way from home.

The air goes in. My shoulders lift. I exhale.
So. Not today. I walk back, look up "suicide" in the phone book, and dial the crisis center number.

∾

IN THE WEEKS that pass, a sense of the possible slowly returns. Eventually it occurs to me that after four years in the conservatory and decades of training in classical music, what gets me through the dark days is not Schubert lieder, but the songs of slaves.

What right do I have to their sorrow, their jubilation? They were abducted, beaten, sold, denied their humanity. My belly is full. My skin is white. They were not my ancestors, but rather Jettie's. Big and brown, she came to our house three times a week when I was little. She had an enormous bosom and wore a white uniform. She smelled steamy clean like the ironing. Jettie fed me hush puppies—wonderful concoctions of cornmeal, eggs, and milk. I never thought to wonder who took care of *her* children.

Do I insult her and her ancestors, by wrapping myself in their poetry? This music has the power to heal me. I need to know why.

I, who run from stories of torture, pour over John Lovell's academic and passionate tome *Black Song: The Forge and the Flame*. I find references that expose my ignorance—like Nat Turner, who led "the most successful of the slave rebellions." (When William Styron's novelization of Turner's story won the 1968 Pulitzer Prize, I was only seventeen, oblivious to both the novel and the ensuing furor.) Now I follow Nat Turner from *Black Song* to the encyclopedias—*The World Book, Britannica, The Encyclopedia of Black America*. Depending on the source consulted, Turner's followers "massacred," "murdered," or simply "killed," "fifty-five" to "several hundred" white adults and children, more than any other rebellion. But most of his followers were massacred in turn. Turner was caught and hanged. And the backlash against slaves who had nothing to do with the rebellion was horrific. So how was he successful? He destroyed the cherished myth of the content slave. He made sorrow and rage indisputably visible.

Teach me, teach me why the slaves sang, and how they kept singing.

Of African descent, they were story finders and storytellers. Some risked retribution and learned to read—from the master's children, from lawbreaking whites. The Bible was their primer. There they found, not religion, the books tell me, so much as stories, stories that they could teach to others, stories that they could sing. They were selective. There are few Christmas spirituals, many about the crucifixion. They built their own poetic mythology from the Bible's heroes (Moses, David, Joshua) and places (the river Jordan, the promised land of Canaan).

On the surface, these were the master's own stories, so how could he forbid the singing of them? But below the surface, the slaves expressed their sadness, joy, longing, hopes, dreams, and assertion of their humanity. And deeper still they sent coded messages that told when it was time to join the Underground Railroad ("Steal Away") and how to reach the promised land of freedom ("Follow the Drinking Gourd"). All resistance fighters must learn to disguise their intent, but these invested their coded messages with such profound beauty it takes my breath away.

I turn from books to people, black and white: singers, researchers, arrangers, and leaders of ensembles. I catch their urgency. The generation that learned spirituals from their grandparents is dying. Time is running out.

They tell me, "If you want to know about spirituals, you must talk to Sylvia Olden Lee. She knows. She coached Kathleen Battle and Jessye Norman for *Spirituals in Concert*—the 1990 performance at Carnegie Hall that made a statement to the classical music world: Spirituals are 'real' music, not some kind of dessert to be dressed up in Hollywood arrangements and served at the end of the annual high school chorus concert. Talk to Ms. Lee."

Sylvia Olden Lee is such a tiny woman. She has pale skin and red wavy hair that comes down to a square jaw. Her features are European rather than African. (Her mother, she says, looked "exactly like Farrah Fawcett" and was offered a position at the Met on the condition that she "pass—give up being colored." She refused.)

Ms. Lee has been accompanying and coaching (teaching song interpretation) since she graduated from the Oberlin Conservatory of Music in 1938. Much of her classical music career was spent in Scandinavia, although she also held staff positions at the Curtis Institute of Music and the Metropolitan Opera. (She taught in a summer institute at the Met six months before Marian Anderson publicly broke the color barrier. She was told that she could not be on the regular season's staff because she was a woman.) When I spoke to her she was living in Philadelphia and commuting one day a week to Washington to teach at Howard University.

She *sounds* like a vocal coach. Her voice is high and light—filled with energy. She is seventy-six, but there is no quaver to her voice when she illustrates a point by singing, and every note is in tune. The words "*won*derful" and "*mar*velous" are sprinkled throughout her conversation. She punctuates these with italics, her voice shooting up at least a fifth, and then glissando-ing down. Affection and pride warm her voice when she talks about how hard "the girls" worked to soften their classical English diction into the Southern dialect appropriate for spirituals. (The girls are opera stars Kathleen Battle and Jessye Norman.)

"My great-grandfather on my father's side was born a slave. His mother (who was part Cherokee) with her eleven or twelve children was put out on that Trail of Tears in 1838 or so to move from South Carolina and push their way to reservations in Oklahoma and Arizona. She got to Nashville, and she said 'I can't go no further, and they can't make me.' So she squatted there. And the kids were split up and they were bought. A kindly couple bought my great-grandfather. They took him and put him out to the white church and made him a sexton. They went against the law and taught him how to read and write. The couple made the stipulation that when they died he would be free. His daughter grew up free and went to Fisk University. She was one of the first graduates, and one of the Fisk Jubilee Singers, who toured this country and Europe singing spirituals to raise the funds to build Fisk University.

"At Fisk my grandmother met my grandfather, who was born a slave. He had belonged to the Oldham Plantation near Louisville. He was twelve or fourteen years old when the war broke out. He ran away so he could fight. He went to the border of Ohio and swam the creek that's the Ohio River at that point. He was too young, so they had him as a water boy. But then things got really bad and they let him fight. Then Mr. Lincoln comes forth and frees everybody in 1863 and he goes off back home. And he needs a name and he thought, 'Oldham was a pretty decent master, so I'll take his name, but I'm not going to spell it that darn way. I'm going to spell it Olden.'

"More than a hundred years later, I was up in St. Louis playing for Bob McFerrin, the opera singer, and his son Bobby, who got so famous singing jazz. They both got honorary doctorates. There was a note in the program: 'Mr. and Mrs. Oldham have donated a chair to the University of St. Louis.' So at the reception afterwards, I met them. They were an interracial couple. She looked like Diana Ross and he was the clone of Carroll O'Connor: He looked just like Archie Bunker.

"So I went up to them and I said, 'Mr. Oldham, did you perhaps spring from the Oldham county plantation in Kentucky?'

"He said, 'Yes.'

"I said, 'My grandfather was a slave on your plantation. Shake hands, cousin.' "

∞

SOMETIMES songs choose you. Once chosen, what right do you have to deny them your voice?

Besides, I may be making distinctions that music itself would find irrelevant. In the last movement of Mahler's Second Symphony, the *Resurrection,* the chorus sings:

On wings that I have acquired through suffering will I soar

The unknown composer of "By an' By" expressed the thought this way:

I know my robe's gonna fit me well
I tried it on at the gates of hell

Why would I sing one and not the other?

∞

WHEN MUSIC chooses you, it comes when you need it.

Struggling with bedsheets at two in the morning, tormented

by painful ghosts and an anxious future, I hear a voice gently
rocking:

> *There is a balm*

then rising in hope

> *in Gilead*

and best of all

> *To make the wounded whole*

   I feel a soothing moving around and inside me, easing my
body and my spirit. The voice goes on:

> *Sometimes I feel discouraged,*
> *And think my work's in vain,*
> *But then the Holy Spirit*
> *Revives my soul again.*
>
> *Oh, there is a balm . . .*

And I sleep.

Teach Your Children Well

*M*r. Karlsrud died last month. My first singing teacher. Seventy years old. I did the math: He was forty when I took my first singing lesson at fifteen; he was younger than I am now.

I stood nervously on the thick beige carpet in the Karlsruds' living room. Mrs. Karlsrud smiled encouragingly from the piano. Mr. Karlsrud instructed and sang in his booming bass. A big man, big presence, big voice. Pale skin from indoor rehearsals. When he took a deep breath, his whole torso expanded—front, sides, and back—puffed out like a bullfrog. Fascinating. My first songs were: *"Caro mio ben,"* to teach me legato line; "As Long As He Needs Me," for its "ee" vowels; and Burleigh's arrangement of "Were You There When They Crucified My Lord?" not because of its heartbreaking beauty, but because it might come in handy getting an Easter church gig.

He made a living that supported a family of five in West-
chester County, New York, and he did it by singing—recitals, a
church job, a synagogue job, and ensemble work when I first
knew him, then later as a minor soloist at the Met.

Lesson 1. Music is business, serious business.

∾

SENIOR YEAR of high school, I went to see his first performance at
the "new Met," in the newly built Lincoln Center. A glittering,
glamorous opera house, with Chagall murals shining down on the
fountain in the square. The grand overture of Wagner's *Die Meister-
singer* began, transporting me to the story of a cobbler winning love
and a singing competition, against a richly colored landscape of sight
and sound where every event moved slowly and every character
seemed enormous. The twelve "mastersingers" strode onto the
stage in black robes that he'd told me were real velvet. The robes
were heavy and hot, but, by God, they draped. I couldn't tell
which one he was. Disappointment and pride and five hours of
Wagner. Quite an afternoon for a girl brought up on *My Fair Lady*.

He'd worked and waited until the Met offered him a solo role
rather than chorus, an approach consonant with the discipline
that permeated everything he did. Before the Met, he'd managed
one of the ensembles he sang in. Any singer who was late to one
of his rehearsals was docked a dollar a minute—three times the
cost of a loaf of bread for one minute's tardiness.

Lesson 2. God forgives all sins but being late to rehearsal.

∾

MR. SLATER taught piano. He was in his late thirties when I was
in high school. Tall, gangly, pale. (They all seem to be pale.)

Round moon of a face. A man of many jobs. Band director at Mamaroneck High, where he had a dance band. Played jazz gigs on the weekend. Taught a few piano students. Taught jazz at the Dance, Drama, Music Workshop—my mother's school.

He walked into the workshop one afternoon, despondent. "Joyce . . ." (that was my mom) "Joyce, the dance band, I screamed at them. I made them miserable. Not because they were bad. They were so close, so close to being great that I forgot they were kids and I pushed them too hard."

Lesson 3. Even teachers make mistakes.

∾

MY PIANO lessons were in a tiny, paneled room in his house. Toilet seat hanging over the door, painted with a circle of gay flowers, a present from his high school kids. A sign above it read, ESCAPE WHILE THERE'S STILL TIME.

Bach, Haydn, Chopin, Czerny, "Fly Me to the Moon," "Tangerine," "Tenderly." The old standards. Nowadays this is no big deal, what with Bobby McFerrin conducting the Saint Paul Chamber Orchestra and Plácido Domingo recording show tunes. But in the sixties, classical was classical and jazz was jazz and you did not cross over.

Lesson 4. It's all music.

∾

BASIC THEORY, the scales in all their versions. Jazz tunes with a melody line above, chords by the number (I, IV, V_7) below, so I wouldn't just play the chord, I'd learn the structure. Bach inventions: study counterpoint. The *Well Tempered Clavier:* learn to write fugues. Hindemith, Debussy, Persichetti: fingers and brain absorbing their vocabulary of sounds, the way they structured their pieces. Right up through Schönberg and 12 tone.

Lesson 5. If you're going to make music, you'd better understand it.

ᐁ

MR. SLATER suggested I learn an ensemble instrument one summer. "How about string bass? Girls don't usually play that." Clever man.

So orchestra opened to me and concert band. Since my small school had no tuba, I filled in the bass line sawing away at my strings. I even tried marching band—playing the glockenspiel—but we didn't have a proper harness and the flag holder we used hurt my neck.

What an education in musicianship.

The world talks about singers and *musicians,* not singers and instrumentalists. The insult has some basis in truth. Singers often start lessons at fifteen or sixteen, when the voice has settled down. (Many teachers consider it healthier since not only boys, but also girls, can find their voices doing quirky things as they head into adolescence.) Pianists and violinists are often hard at it by the age of three. So unless a singer also plays an instrument, he or she may head out into the world a decade behind in learning what makes up music. Some of us never make up the deficit. Pushed by some teachers to—above all—sound and look pretty, singers have a reputation for thinking the piece is over when they've sung their last note, even though the orchestra plays on.

I'm grateful that I was taught to value the composer's intentions and given the tools for discovering them.

I'm grateful, too, that there was money for lessons. I wish every musical child—the brilliant and the moderately talented—could be so blessed.

∿

ON TO THE Oberlin Conservatory, where they assigned me Doris Mayes. Chocolate brown skin, generous bosom, shapely legs below the short skirts of her suits. A dark mezzo sound. My voice got heavier imitating her. I lost light, high notes that I would regain four years later in postgraduate study with Marlene Rosen. That first year at Oberlin, I ignored the friends who told me, "Switch to Mr. Hatton or Mr. Miller. You'll get such a fine technique." I liked Miss Mayes's laugh. And when I wanted to sing Rodgers and Hart on my senior recital—so that my dad could hear some of the music he loved—Miss Mayes said, "Fine."

The rest of the voice faculty was not so agreeable. They said they would try to block my graduation if I put Richard Rodgers on my program. Scott Joplin had just crept into the classical piano canon, thanks to the New England Conservatory Ragtime Ensemble, but the voice teachers (afraid of being called "singers" instead of "musicians"?) held firm.

The music theater director, David Bamberger, advised, "Don't put the show tunes on your program. Sing them as encores."

Lesson 6. When caught between a rock and a hard place, become thin and slippery.

∿

DAVID HAD worked as an assistant director under Gian Carlo Menotti (composer of *Amahl and the Night Visitors*). David said that Menotti had said, "If you have to choose between drama and purity of sound in my operas, choose drama." The voice faculty didn't care for David.

After my recital, David told me, "I had no idea what your father looked like. But it turned out I was sitting behind him. He lit up like a thousand-watt lightbulb when you came out and sang "To Keep My Love Alive."

Lesson 7. Music is a gift to be given away, even when the authorities try to stop you.

∾

THE EARLY lessons stick. At thirty-eight I auditioned to study with a new teacher, a well-known performer, just moved to Minnesota from New York. A privilege, I was told, if she accepted me.

When we got to the end of the audition-cum-lesson, she said, "Oh, and if you study with me, you cannot sing anything but classical."

"Cannot? You mean I'm not supposed to sing show tunes in my living room?"

"That's exactly what I mean. I started out singing Country Western and it almost ruined my voice, so I know whereof I speak." (She actually said "whereof.")

Clearly, her Lesson 4 was different from mine. I respectfully declined and went out and found Marian Hoffman.

I have come to lessons full of questions from long hours of practice and experimentation. I've shown up barely prepared. I've arrived healthy and vibrant, stuffed with a cold, or dealing with menstrual cramps that give an extra big twinge every time I take a deep breath. Given the ingredients of a joyful, energized, exhausted, or grieving student, Marian has always created an hour of upbeat learning, and given me something new to take home.

∞

MUSIC lessons come in handy at the oddest times.

I had talked my way into a job writing business plans. I was faking it and knew it. I could read a score of a Mozart symphony but not an annual report. I figured an MBA program would be a good place to learn. But by the end of the first week of classes the only things I was sure I had learned were (a) what hell felt like and (b) how profoundly I was going to fail there.

I'd splashed black ink all over a cream silk blazer when my pen exploded in class. I'd been defeated by my computer terminal because the university computer center had changed all the access codes without bothering to inform the business school. I'd been crushed into a helpless blob of stupidity by my first math class since high school—statistics.

I walked up to Professor Norm Chervany at the end of the last statistics class of that first week and calmly informed him "I'm going to need some help." Then burst into tears.

I ran for the ladies' room. Cold water to face. Deep breaths. (Singers know a lot about deep breaths.) I squared my shoulders, lifted my head, and walked back to face him. He looked more embarrassed than I felt.

"Don't worry," he said. "I'll work with you till you get it. And you will get it."

Right.

Two tutoring sessions later, I could execute the mechanics. Without any comprehension, it's true, but still an inch of progress. Then, the night before session #3, lightning flashed and, by its peculiar illumination, I saw, really *saw* the statistical curve. A pattern expressing an idea. New information modifies its shape, but the curve somehow retains its identity. In a way I cannot explain, these modifications of one core idea reminded me of a Bach fugue: subject, countersubject, transposition, inversion.

Look at the curve, then read the narrative, then attack the formula. I could do that. Curve, words, formulas. Notes, words, phrases. Harmony, rhythm, melody. Break it down into the elements. Find the commonality.

I called Norm to cancel next morning's tutoring.

"Well," he said, "that's a bit sooner than I expected, but I knew you'd get it."

What did I learn from the music teachers?

Lesson 8. The best lesson of all. I learned how to learn.

A Peace as
Audible as War

*M*ONDAY, MAY 4, 1970. OBERLIN, OHIO. Twenty miles or so from the practice room where I sing scales, National Guardsmen shoot and kill four students protesting the Vietnam War. They were throwing rocks at the Guard, the newspapers said. Sure. Big, heavy, dangerous rocks, like you frequently find littering campus grounds—dangerous enough to warrant the retaliation of a bullet. The nation will remember the cover of *Life*—the young woman on one knee, her hand outstretched, pointing, her mouth open in a scream. I remember the stone steps of the Conservatory: white, hard, cool. I sat and stared at the pretty, Ivy League picture described by the college square: smooth grass and lush trees, thinking *They're shooting at students just like me—nice girls from the suburbs. They're shooting at* me. The war had come home.

SUNDAY, MAY 10, 1970. WASHINGTON, D.C.

"Dies irae! Dies illa!" Rage and grief pour into the cavern of the National Cathedral. Two hundred sixty-four professors and students: timpani pounding, strings attacking, voices crying out.

The Kent State students had been murdered six days ago, Monday. Tuesday, we had wandered the crisscross of paths from building to building: encountering, grouping, murmuring a few short sentences, then moving on, our stunned shock gradually transforming into a need to do something, something with this energy of horror. Classes were canceled. Grades—the measure of some distant fairy tale life—were frozen. Even senior recitals (that sacred final exam of music students) were postponed. Students—mostly from the College of Liberal Arts—began to bustle about, planning the huge protest in D.C.

But was there something else we in the Conservatory could do, should do, as musicians? Wednesday afternoon, we met in the chorus rehearsal room. Someone suggested we perform the Mozart *Requiem*. Someone gathered the orchestra, making sure all parts were filled; someone asked faculty members to sing the solos; someone chartered seven buses for the fourteen-hour ride—though he had to search as far afield as Dearborn, Michigan, to find any that were available. Someone found the music; someone made the armbands. Someone called Richard W. Dirksen of the National Cathedral and convinced him not only to make room for our performance on a weekend that already included four weddings and nine Sunday services but also to find us lodging for the night.

So many someones. Invisible to me then. I am grateful to them now. Someone publicized the concert so that people might actually show up.

Me, I learned notes. Learned notes and made toast. I landed

a cafeteria job substituting for someone organizing the big protest, the rally at the Ellipse. I placed squishy white bread on the odd conveyor belt toaster and smelled the steamy cafeteria smell and felt the oddness of this time-out-of-time, this extraordinary finale to my freshman year.

Three days of rehearsal to prepare one of the great choral works. Most of the kids had never seen a note of it before. We sang three rehearsals a day, two to three hours each. To put a chorus through that and have them come out at the other end with voices strong and vibrant is an enormous achievement. Conductor Robert Fountain accomplished it while downing sugary drinks to keep up his energy. He'd been feeling tired lately. He learned later that it was the onset of diabetes.

Decades later, a recording stands as testament to the quality of that performance: Rock solid. Clean and clear. Tempos slow enough to adjust for the reverberation: The final note of any movement takes a full three seconds to decay and finally come to silence in the great space of the National Cathedral.

That Sunday we stood in rows as regimented as any battalion. Our uniform: black pants or skirts, white shirts, and every left sleeve encircled with a black armband. Ushers offered armbands to each listener as well. "What does the red circle on it stand for?" asked one. "Mourning, peace, moving forward," came the reply. The audience donned that part of our uniform. Then they formed their quiet rank and file and opened their hearts to us.

After the terrified *Dies Irae*, we live the confusion of the *Confutatis*, the mourning *Lacrymosa*, the lilting comfort of the *Hostias*, finally arriving at the prayer: "Eternal rest grant to them, O Lord, and let perpetual light shine upon them, in the company of Thy saints forever because Thou art forgiving." *Quia pius es.*

We sing the final chord, the open fifth, neither major nor minor. No promise of paradise, but no resignation into hell, either. An unanswered question. The sound softens for a split second, almost hesitating. Then grows and grows over timpani rumbling into thunder. Cutoff. The pitches, now separate from our bodies, hang suspended in space. No one moves. No one breathes. Just as the chord approaches silence, the Cathedral bells begin to toll. Bong. Bong. Low and slow. Steady. An answer of sorts. An acknowledgment that we had been heard.

∾

WHO AM I to comment on war and peace? What right has a woman who has never known combat duty, who avoids protests because she doesn't like crowds? Better, perhaps, to hear from my father who served in World War II, or my friend Jim, who spent his Vietnam years accompanying the corpses of Marines home, because, his sergeant told him, he *looks* like a Marine should look: tall and solid. Better to hear from my Uncle Ray who never became my uncle because he left Canada to join the RAF and went down with his plane. (God, how I would like to hear from my Uncle Ray.) But if people like me, the civilians, the casual peaceniks, content ourselves with smiling sweetly as we hand out flowers and sing "All we are saying / is give peace a chance"—if we do not consider war as part of the human condition, or acknowledge the attraction of violence—we consign our fates to the politicians and generals. I am unwilling.

∾

WHEN YOU say "the war" to a gathering of my parents and their friends, they know exactly what you're talking about. As do I and my friends, when you use the same phrase with us. Only they mean World War II and we mean Vietnam. Thus generations are defined.

∞

HEAR THE bugle's blare; the fife's shrill cry, the drum beating, beating, raising spirits on the battlefront and at home. "When Johnny comes marching home again, hurrah! hurrah!" Johnny is sure to march home again—of course he is—so he can go into battle a little more easily.

Is music a weapon of war? Of course.

Caesar's troops are rumored to have marched to salacious ditties about their commanding officers' less attractive proclivities. Soldiers throughout history have sung to give their dog-tired bodies energy, to give themselves courage when they were scared beyond all admitting, to let off steam, to build camaraderie, for simple entertainment. The people on the homefront sang for all the same reasons and to connect with their "boys."

A lot of good tunes have refused to take sides. Johnny came marching home both above and below the Mason-Dixon Line during the Civil War, and he marched through time into even greater popularity during the Spanish-American War more than three decades later. "Lili Marlene" was sung by the Allies and the Axis troops during World War II. Both, naturally, claimed her as their own.

Like the crafters of hymns and folk songs, soldiers and their kinfolk appropriated both melodies and words that served their purposes. Sometimes not changing the words—"Dixie" was written by a Northerner. Sometimes parodying songs—an enemy's or even their own, if the song was too reverent for the needs of the moment. (During World War I, soldiers were heard to render

"Over there, over there" as "Underwear, underwear.") Sometimes the songmakers took a current tune and gave it new words. Julia Ward Howe's words, "Mine eyes have seen the glory of the coming of the Lord," are sung to the same tune as "John Brown's body lies a-mouldering in the grave." So "The Battle Hymn of the Republic" appropriated its melody from "John Brown's Body." But Union troops had only recently appropriated Mr. Brown's melody themselves from a Southern camp-meeting hymn.

Possibly the most egregious melodic retrofit is "The Star Spangled Banner." Francis Scott Key wrote the words during the War of 1812. He witnessed the all-night bombardment of Fort McHenry, and at dawn saw the Stars and Stripes still floating above the fort. Flooded with joy and relief, he scribbled the words on an envelope. (Between this incident and the Gettysburg Address, American history seems to owe a lot to the practice of carrying around old envelopes.)

Key took the lyrics back home with him to Baltimore and had handbill copies printed and distributed. We don't know exactly how the words of "The Star Spangled Banner" came to be sung to the tune of a then-popular English drinking song, "To Anacreon in Heaven." The tune had already been appropriated for several patriotic songs. Key may have suggested it, as the meter and structure of the two sets of lyrics match pretty well. Think of the last two lines of the first verse of our anthem ("Oh say, does that Star Spangled Banner yet wave . . .") and try singing the last two lines of the original's first verse:

> *And besides I'll instruct you, like me, to entwine*
> *The myrtle of Venus with Bacchus's vine.*

The notes that give the average person such trouble at a baseball stadium would have posed no problem in the original. The opening "Oh-oh say can you see" works perfectly if you slide the "Oh-oh" like you're drunk. The high fanfare of "And the rocket's red glare" (the part where most people drop down an octave) would have posed no problem in the local tavern since neither singer nor audience would have been in any shape to notice inaccuracy. Despite its greater suitability for inebriated singers, the melody joined forces forever with Key's poem about victory in war to become our national anthem.

Something happened to war songs when the "war to end all wars" became World War I. In his book *American Popular Song*, Alec Wilder speaks of a growing cynicism among the young: "The innocence, the slogans, the idealism had vanished. An 'Over There' would have been jeered at this trip." George M. Cohan's lyrics had proclaimed joyfully "the Yanks are coming . . . And we won't come back till it's over over there." But such gay bravado is rarely to be found in the songs of the World War II years. Writing from the perspective of the early seventies, Wilder continues: "There was too much cynicism among the young. The big, impersonal war machine had taken over and everyone knew it. . . . There will be no mention in this study of World War II songs."

Maybe innocence had disappeared (although every generation believes in the innocence of the preceding one), but how can Wilder so harshly and abruptly dismiss such great World War II songs as: "God Bless America," "I Left My Heart at the Stage Door Canteen," "Comin' in on a Wing and a Prayer," and the tender, hopeful "White Cliffs of Dover"?

There'll be blue birds over
The white cliffs of Dover
Tomorrow, just you wait and see.

There'll be love and laughter
And peace ever after
Tomorrow, when the world is free.

Wilder is correct that as the nature of war changed in the twentieth century, so did the music making that surrounded it.

Protest songs and "peace hymns" had been sung in this country at least since our War of Independence, but only with Korea did they become prominent features in the landscape of popular culture. A few songs—mostly country and western—glorified the Korean "conflict," but the tune that has endured from that period is Ed McCurdy's folk song "Last Night I Had the Strangest Dream":

Last night I had the strangest dream
I'd never dreamed before
I dreamed the world had all agreed
To put an end to war.

During Vietnam a second war took place on radio airwaves. The combatants were not so much antiwar and pro-war, as antiwar, pro-war, and antiprotester. Folk and rock stations played John Lennon's "All we are saying is give peace a chance." Country-western and Easy Listening stations opposed with views perhaps best expressed by Merle Haggard's "The Fightin' Side of Me":

If you don't love it, leave it.

In the sixties peace songs crossed the divide between folk music and the mainstream: Buffy Saint-Marie's "Universal Soldier" and Donovan's "The War Goes On" made it to the Top 40 charts. But after Vietnam we pretty much stopped singing. Sure, we tied yellow ribbons around trees to bring our hostages home from Iran, heard radio stations playing a childish adaptation of "Barbara Ann" with the words changed to "Bomb Iran." But where are the great tunes from the Falklands Islands conflict? Operation Desert Storm? If Wilder thought World War II was fought by "an impersonal war machine," he should see how we're fighting now.

JANUARY 1991. MINNEAPOLIS, MINNESOTA.

I am driving downtown to Orchestra Hall, traveling through the darkness of an early winter evening. Warming up. Long hums and glissandos. "La la la la la." I turn on the radio. Iraq. The bombs have begun to fall—I can hear them—in this TV-show war where no one gets hurt. No one because the Iraqis aren't people, they're debris or something. I wear a warm coat over my Chorale uniform and the heater in my car is in good working order but I can't get warm. The bombs are falling in the desert and I am traveling to Orchestra Hall to sing fairy music. *A Midsummer Night's Dream*, Mendelssohn's incidental music to Shakespeare's play. A tiny singing part, just women, just a couple of songs where the fairies serenade their queen, Titania.

White faces in the warm-up room, white, strained faces of those who have loved ones in Israel. Don't fight back, we've asked Israel. Just sit there or the conflict will get bigger. Just sit there and we Americans will protect you from becoming debris.

Not the Mozart *Requiem*. Not the Mahler *Resurrection* symphony. Not something large and meaningful that might lend us insight, nobility, comfort. Do we sing this piece tonight? Flutter around the forest of Arden with King Oberon and his puckish assistant? The orchestra was meeting to decide. Adjuncts, incidental blackbirds with white faces, we flutter and wait. Yes. They will broadcast the president's announcement at 8:00 P.M. to those who actually show up for the concert, and then begin. The strings will *hee haw* as the weaver Bottom turns into a donkey. Mendelssohn's famous wedding march will ring out.

What does it matter? How could it possibly matter, whether we sing a chord in tune? I say it does. I say that each passionate, precise note is an act of defiance and a prayer. Human creatures can create, destroy, or sink into numbness. These seem to me the choices. I love the bumper sticker MUSIC CAN SAVE THE WORLD. Not because it is true. I have never believed it to be true. But because it's a damn sight better standard to bear than "Let's drop a few bombs for peace."

The orchestra had hired an actress from the Guthrie Theater—Kelly Burton Shaw—to read some of Shakespeare's lines, to give the audience a sense of what the incidental music was incidental to. She faces out into the half-empty concert hall, a petite woman, wearing a backless, black evening gown. From our risers, we singers cannot see her face. We hear her voice conveying each character in turn—harsh Oberon, glittering Titania, impish Puck, foolish Bottom. The muscles over her shoulder blades shift attitude with each new character. We enchant our fairy queen: "Lulla, lulla, lullaby . . ." (elongating the "u" so it sounds like

"LOO-luh-bye") "so good night, with lullaby." Not relevant, but not difficult to sing either.

Then Oberon, finally sated with the swirling chaos of confusion and frustration he has created, sets about restoring order. (That night he was not funny. That night Oberon filled me with rage.) He releases his wife from the humiliating spell that caused her to adore a donkey. Bottom's ass head vanishes and the simple peasant is human again. The resentful lovers sort themselves into loving pairs. And this fairy king, whose mischief and perverse sense of humor have inflicted such pain, bestows a benediction.

> *With this field dew consecrate,*
> *Every fairy take his gait,*
> *And each several chamber bless,*
> *Through this palace, with sweet peace.*
> *Ever shall in safety rest,*
> *And the owner of it blest.*

The actress paused the length of a heartbeat before the words "sweet peace." Shakespeare's skillful comedy, this bit of amusing fluff, had given us the prayer we needed that night.

∾

MUSIC CAN pray for peace. It can carry gallant soldiers into righteous battle. Therefore, we might well conclude that music is a force for good. Unfortunately, such a conclusion fails the test of history. Music is indeed a force, but its pure power lacks ethics. Beauty can be twisted into beastliness.

As Henry Oertelt tells it, the Nazis rounded up musicians, actors, artists, intellectuals, clergy and sent them to the

Theresienstadt concentration camp in Czechoslovakia. An announcement went round that a choir of inmates was to be formed to perform Haydn's *Creation*. "My brother and I applied," he says, "and, since we were tenors, of course we got in." Choirs always need tenors, it seems, even in concentration camps. The camp commandant promised that all performers would be safe from the ongoing deportations to Auschwitz. This made the hours of rehearsal especially sweet, even after the long, hard working days. Occasionally performers did disappear, but with that pool of talent, they were easily replaced, and the performance was a success. Then, wonder of wonders, they began rehearsing Mendelssohn's *Elijah*. Performing the music of Mendelssohn—who was born a Jew but whose father had him baptized in the Lutheran church when he was seven—was forbidden throughout German-controlled territory.

To perform not just Mendelssohn, but his *Elijah*. The piece begins with a short proclamation by the prophet. Then an overture. Fine. But then the chorus of inmates would cry out, anguished and loud, "Help, Lord! Help, Lord! Wilt thou quite destroy us? The people of Israel are starving. There is no water. The children cry out for bread and there is no one to give it to them."

The Nazis sat listening, the commander and his uniformed SS cohorts right beside the leaders of the Jewish prisoners.

I asked Oertelt how he felt singing those words in that place. I was sure he would say bitter, betrayed by the God who had abandoned him there. Instead, his face shines. "Wonderful. It felt wonderful, to sing exactly what we felt." But then, "There was supposed to be a second performance. We were so looking forward to it. But it was canceled. We only found out later that they were filming us." The Nazis had got the footage they needed on the first take. Enough to show the world how the "resettled" Jews were living in cultural luxury. "A few days later, I found most of my co-performers lined up with my brother and me, being driven by gun butts and sticks into cattle cars destined for Auschwitz."

The filmed performance added to the Nazi's arsenal of propaganda. But still, the music makers knew that for a few moments they had sung truth. And some of them lived to tell about it.

FRIDAY, NOVEMBER 1995. TEMPLE ISRAEL, MINNEAPOLIS, MINNESOTA. This was supposed to be a service of remembrance and peace, a coming together of secular and sacred choirs to commemorate the fiftieth anniversary of the end of World War II. But all that changed when Yitzhak Rabin was shot the Saturday before.

What I hate most is the thought of the blood-soaked song sheet. They were at a peace rally. Shimon Perez says that Rabin never sang in public. "I'm not a singer," Rabin would say. It takes courage to sing, when you don't think you have a voice. But this time he consented to. He and the other dignitaries stood in a semi-circle around a blonde, busty woman with a microphone, holding their song sheets in their hands. And then Rabin neatly folded the sheet and put it in his pocket—his breast pocket—and walked out into the night and the bullet went through his jacket and spilled blood on the paper and killed him.

We have come to Temple Israel to sing Leonard Bernstein's *Chichester Psalms,* and now we are also here to sing *"Shir LaShalom"* from our copies of that song sheet. Bernstein would have understood. His boy soprano, the young psalmist David, sings the lovely, pastoral "The Lord is my shepherd," only to be interrupted by the men's chorus shouting, "Why do the nations rage?" Back and forth they go, the peaceful, the raucous, until finally the boy soars above. Peace at last. But no, not quite. Low, in the distance the men's chorus still menaces, muttering.

At the hospital, they gave the song sheet to Eitan Haber, director of the prime minister's office. He brought it to the funeral so we could all see, through the eyes of TV cameras at least. Carefully, neatly enclosed in plastic sheeting, the blood was a sash of red across the middle of the page, lines of Hebrew above and below. Rabin sang a bit out of tune, Haber said.

It is beyond singing, but what else is there to do? What difference can music make in a world of blood-soaked song sheets? Nothing changes, thousands of years and nothing changes.

But at least we are together, at least we do not mourn alone. Survivors of "the Good War" stand with their grandchildren. People who have never attended a Shabbat service in their lives stand next to people who have never spent Friday night anywhere but a synagogue.

For once in my performing life I can cry when I sing. Vocal quality is hardly an issue tonight. Rabin had the courage to sing for us, so now we raise our voices to sing the sadly prophetic *"Shir LaShalom"* for him: "Sing a song of peace for those who have fallen. Tears, prayers and words of praise will not return them to life, but peace will sanctify their deaths."

∞

WHEN YOU think about it, it's surprising that we have a word "peace" in the English language. "Nonwar" would do—our vision of the condition is so blurry. Once peace was a time between, a cluster of years when the nations of the world stopped trying to destroy each other for a while. But now it's hard to say. When a few of our soldiers are "policing" small distant areas of the globe, are we at peace or war? Nuclear annihilation seems less of an immediate threat than it did during the Cold War, but is this the best peace we can hope for?

If peace is going to be more than nonwar, we are going to have to make it, quite deliberately. For that, we must have a sense of what we are making.

In "The Warrior," an article in *Esquire,* July 1986, George Leonard writes about our need for hero warriors and about the attraction of war. Leonard served as a combat pilot in World War II and an air intelligence officer during the Korean "conflict." He later achieved a third-degree black belt in aikido, a martial art dedicated to harmony.

"The problem is not that war is so often vivid, but that peace is so often drab," Leonard asserts. He tells of a friend for whom "the smell of a cup of coffee in a snow-covered German forest is more real, even now, forty years later than anything in his present surroundings." Of his own recollections, Leonard says, "the unbelieving, strangely amused look on the pilot's face in the plane next to me as his windscreen was shattered by ground fire just north of Manila remains as marvelously crystal-clear today as it was then."

Leonard argues that we will not sustain lasting peace until we find a way to create "a peace that is not only just, but also vivid," a peace that engages our passion and pushes us to our limits.

MARCH 1989. CAPE COD, MASSACHUSETTS.
CLOP clop, CLOP clop. I'm wrapped up in a scratchy woolen blanket, the hard wood of a hay wagon under my cold fanny. The occasional snowflake melts on my nose. Present at this event are

my sister and brother-in-law, their three children, a few neighbors, the Vietnamese ambassador to the UN, his wife, first secretary, and bodyguard. My brother-in-law had discovered that, since we did not yet have diplomatic relations with Vietnam, Ambassador Trinh Xuan Lang was proscribed to a limit of twenty-five miles in circumference from the UN buildings in Manhattan.

"This is crazy!" Joe had proclaimed. A founding member of Vietnam Vets Against the War in Philadelphia, he declared the twenty-five-mile limit "a lost opportunity for creating greater understanding between our two countries." He instigated an invitation issued by his Unitarian Universalist church to host an ambassadorial visit to the small town of Brewster, Massachusetts. (With a general store and a proper New England church—small, white, and steepled—Brewster may lie only a six-hour drive from New York, but the distance seems like light-years.) Joe petitioned the State Department to allow the visit. In the petition, Joe wrote that the ambassador's visit would make Joe happy, and as an American, he had the inalienable right to the pursuit of happiness. The State Department formed a committee, pondered it for two days, and finally approved "Operation Spring Thaw."

I'm just visiting from out of town, so I'm not invited to the more formal events, but "Sure, come on the hayride." Joe speaks Vietnamese, as he does a couple of languages, with great enthusiasm and enough accuracy that no one winces. The ambassador and First Secretary Dzung speak English, of course, but the ambassador's wife, Ngo Thi Hong, seems not to, or is shy. At any rate, a silence falls. We hear the horses' hooves, the slight squeaking of the wagon, and then a light, Irish tenor voice. His hands chucking the reins, the stable owner has begun singing "Danny Boy." Suddenly, amazingly, we are all singing, even Mrs.

Ambassador. First Secretary Dzung begins "Yankee Doodle." He learned it in English class. Goodness. Joe begins "This Land Is Your Land" and introduces me to a few Leftist verses that never made it into my school songbook.

So we sing, huddled in our blankets, and watch the clouds darken as night falls, and acquire cold, wet noses. The next day at the farewell speeches, Mr. Dzung said that the visit contained surprises. From his experiences in New York, he had concluded that Americans are a formal people. Now seeing them in their homes, he thought perhaps not. But the most significant part of his visit had been the hayride. During the war, he had served as the mathematician at a surface-to-air missile site. While he was watching the bombs fall on Hanoi, he had never dreamed he would be sitting in a horse-drawn wagon with his former enemies, singing.

Peace begins here, I think, when we commit acts of music—crazy and human, like taking an ambassador on a hayride. But maybe we shouldn't wait for a war and its aftermath. What if we made music a tool for resolving everyday conflicts so blood is less likely to flow?

This may be naive and ridiculous, but what if we began each tough negotiation—between the parties in a divorce, between labor and union—by singing a round. It doesn't have to be *"Dona Nobis Pacem"* if that's too difficult. "Row, row, row your boat" will do. And we impose the rule that negotiations cannot commence until the combatants sing the round *well*. "Well" does not mean pretty. We want every voice, harsh or lovely, to take part. But we do require each voice to listen and blend while remaining independent, thus practicing an alternative mode of being in such situations.

Is this crazier than spending weeks negotiating the shape of the meeting room's table? The next time an orchestra goes on strike, why couldn't management and union representatives begin by making music—the ostensible purpose for their professional existence—before tearing at each other like rampaging soldiers? Why the hell not?

∽

In August 1999, near the site of the Buchenwald concentration camp, conductor Zubin Mehta risked leading an orchestra that combined musicians from the Bavarian State Orchestra and the Israel Philharmonic. Only hours before the performance, Mehta and many of the musicians toured the camp, where more than fifty thousand people died between 1937 and 1945. They played Mahler's *Resurrection* symphony—from the funeral march of the first movement through the final victory of the spirit embodied in the choral finale (one line of which can be translated "On wings I have acquired through suffering will I soar").

While Mehta was healing the past, making music with mature players from former enemy countries, conductor Daniel Barenboim was working to create a different kind of future in a workshop of young musicians: Palestinians, Lebanese, Syrians, Israelis, and Germans.

"The issue, in the end, in the Middle East is how to be together," Barenboim said. "Music is an ideal form of communication because it can bring an almost ecstatic togetherness and elevation while remaining essentially abstract."

Seventy ambitious orchestra musicians—most of them in their twenties—rehearsed together and talked. They, too, visited

Buchenwald. Some of the Arab musicians had never heard the words "Holocaust" or "concentration camp" before.

Music can bring us together, but we must also talk about our differences if we are to resolve them. The workshop organizers hired Edward Said, a Palestinian writer and intellectual, to provide his insight into the problems of Arabs and Jews during daily discussions and after the visit to the camp.

A Lebanese violinist said that seeing Buchenwald "did help me, up to a point, understand the feelings of the Jews."

"Up to a point" is honest, and certainly further than he began with. The point may move again—for both Jewish and non-Jewish players—if workshop leaders succeed in their plan for creating an ongoing orchestra from these musicians.

NOVEMBER 4, 1999. ST. PAUL, MINNESOTA.

I have been engaged to sing in "A Peace Concert for the Millennium" at the St. Paul Cathedral, a grand edifice that gazes down Ramsey Hill onto the city of its namesake, which tumbles down to the banks of the Mississippi. The interior is gilded, resonant; the dome high above. We sing music by Bernstein, Bloch, Rachmaninoff, Duruflé, Vaughan Williams—excerpts from longer works: just the lovely parts, the comforting parts. Any loud or strident movements have been deleted. There's none of the terror or confusion experienced in that Mozart *Requiem* decades ago.

I begin the evening full of hope that I'll learn how to study war no more. But as lush phrases follow lyric melodies, energy begins to seep from my body, until I am drained, except for the voice shouting within, "This is not peace. This is sleep."

The tidy inclusion of music written by Jews, Catholics, Russian

Orthodox, and Protestants can't compensate for this disemboweling of the music. It does not nourish—this meal consisting of sweet after sweet. No rage, no fear, no helplessness: no reality.

Soft peace—I can't envision it lasting long. The peace I believe to be possible is full of hard edges, hard choices. A lasting peace will require us to find ways of getting along with people we find despicable (if we are honest enough to admit it), people who think the same of us. Peace will require creativity and compromise, creating a kaleidoscope of exhilaration and tragedy as dreams are fulfilled or dashed. A lasting peace is unlikely to be soothing.

∾

"GOD FORGIVE me but I enjoyed the war," says Sabina in Thornton Wilder's 1942 play *The Skin of Our Teeth*. "Everybody's at their best in wartime. I'm sorry it's over."

War fulfills some human need. Those of us who want peace would be fools not to acknowledge it. Not just the obvious need to defend our lands and loved ones from aggressors. War pushes each of us to our limits—at home and on the front. War unites all of us (however we define "us") against a common enemy. We battle this enemy for our common good. Some part of us wants the drama of war: the thrilling surge of energy, sweaty palms, and sick stomach that signal danger and propel us into exemplary performance during crisis.

A flood can provide such drama. On the news, we see pictures of people from river towns heaving sandbags, battling the rising tide, side by side with convicts from the local penitentiary. Or a child goes missing, and help appears from people who never considered themselves neighbors before. We respond to these crises as a courageous community.

But absent a natural or manmade disaster, few of us choose to abandon our comfortable lives, choose to enter a state of crisis. We could unite to combat diseases, the poverty of children. But in peacetime the nation fragments. We become "us" and "them": rich and poor, young and old, religious liberals and conservatives; all races, creeds, and colors. Divisiveness is an equal opportunity employer. Because they don't get it—the truth that describes our reality. We're sure they never will.

The only enemy we allow to unite us wears a uniform and carries a gun. So we sit on our inertia waiting for a leader to galvanize us into action. Sometimes one does. We race to the moon, then sit back and wonder *What now?* We need to practice living vividly, audaciously—at least some of the time.

When you choose to perform publicly—for your friends or at Carnegie Hall—you are choosing crisis. When you choose to compete—whether your goal is a black belt in aikido or to finish the marathon without throwing up—you are choosing crisis. The risk energizes. The event's date becomes a focal point. You prepare longer, harder, more deeply, with greater attention to detail. For me, the moment before walking onstage feels sacred, clean: *For better or worse, world, this is what I have to give—body, mind, and soul. Now let's see what happens.*

We typically aren't risking our lives with these chosen crises. But our damp palms may not realize that fact. Performance *can* be like combat. So says Don Greene, whose résumé includes: West Pointer, Green Beret and Army Ranger, criminal investigator, and sports psychologist. Greene's current occupation is teaching classical musicians—singers and instrumentalists—how to channel their stage fright into a higher level of performance. He told a *New York Times* reporter, "What the performing arts takes is courage. It's no different from a race car driver or SWAT team member."

We need to use our courage. It gets constipated in front of the TV, in spite of the vicarious combat of football and cop shows. An occasional rush of courage is necessary for us to be fully human.

NOVEMBER 27, 1999. MINNEAPOLIS, MINNESOTA.

A peace as audible as war. I believe I am experiencing the possibility. Beethoven's *Missa Solemnis* is the most profound and difficult work I have ever sung. Imagine the choral bit from his Ninth Symphony extended in every emotional direction—ninety minutes of joy, anguish, terror, comfort. The *Missa Solemnis* asks of us everything and leaves us, well, it's not entirely clear where it leaves us. Certainly with the words *"Dona nobis pacem"* in our mouths.

I am still practicing individual phrases the day of the final performance, something I don't remember doing even for the most merciless of contemporary works. The sopranos have to sing one high B-flat after another—dozens of them. They struggle to keep them in tune and relaxed. The alto part often leaps from pitch to pitch, spanning an octave and a half within one phrase. We strive to focus the collection of pitches into a single, musical line. All parts struggle with the phrases I call "Nasty 1," "Nasty 2," and "Nasty 3," each volley of notes syncopated and so fast the Nasties are almost impossible for even the most skilled vocalist to sing clearly. After six weeks of choral rehearsal, we finally nail Nasty 3 during our first rehearsal with orchestra. What a rush. Absolute, unified precision, each pitch distinct. Why only then? Perhaps in terror that we might disgrace ourselves before the orchestra.

Perhaps in defiance of conductor Harry Bicket, who the day before told us "Just sing that phrase as well as you can and move on."

When Beethoven began to write the *Missa Solemnis,* he was suffering from pain in his eyes, afraid he would lose his sight. His hearing was long gone. Out of this terrifying situation came *"Gloria in excelsis deo,"* a shout of pure joy, fireworks of exaltation. He was about my age. Not a church-going Catholic, his faith—fine and shining—enters me as I sing *"Credo, credo."* I feel the emphasis shift from I *believe* to *I* believe.

Beethoven planned to finish the piece in one year. It took him four. He missed his deadline, and the installation of his patron Archduke Rudolph as Archduke of Olmütz. But over the course of those four years, his visual problems disappeared.

He paints essential human emotion, glowing and dark. As the chorus sings of the crucifixion, we spit the name "Pontius Pilate" and then wail, twisted and sad, on the word *"passus"* (suffered). At last, voice follows voice in fanfare as Jesus is resurrected and ascends to heaven.

Finally, the last movement. We beseech the Lamb of God to have mercy, and then, sure perhaps that our prayer is to be answered, the key switches from minor to major and we dance the words *"Dona nobis pacem,"* grant us peace. The soprano soloist soars. The chorus rings out like the bells on Armistice Day. Silence. There, in the distance, singers and audience alike can barely hear an eerie rumble of drums and crisp bugle calls. The dance is dismissed by a marching beat. The alto soloist pleads *"Agnus Dei"* (Lamb of God). The chorus shouts in fear, "Have mercy on us." The soloists repeat the dance theme. But in the chorus Beethoven quotes the first four notes of "and He shall reign forever and ever" from Handel's "Hallelujah Chorus," which evolves into a more marchlike prayer for peace. March joins dance and together they grow in joy until the bells ring out again. The orchestra interrupts, agitation rising to terror. The chorus shouts its plea to God, then prays for peace.

Four times the drums of war interrupt the prayer—sometimes for a long minute, sometimes for an instant. The chorus is left repeating the word "peace, peace" softly.

The orchestra's music walks forward, gathering momentum and volume. The chorus—the voice of humanity—sings one final phrase. "Grant peace, peace." We are not even asking for ourselves anymore. The final repetitions of "peace" descend to notes that are not high, or loud, or long, but simply stated. A tenuto—a hold—is indicated in the silence *after* the orchestra's final note. Of course Beethoven knew how to end in triumph, as audiences would hear in his Ninth Symphony a year later. Yet he chose not to with the *Missa Solemnis*. Someone asked him, "Why this ending, why not more?"

"I've said what I had to say," Beethoven replied.

Hope, determination, and strength dwell in the prayer that returns time and time again, but no promises. Hope, determination, and strength are quite a lot, really. Beethoven bequeathed us no rosy vision of the future, but the wherewithal to create it: courage to make music. Courage to build a peace as audible as war.

You Can't
Make *Music*

*T*his time it wasn't working. The concert hall was full of people and sound, but so empty. I stood there on the risers, singing my first performance of Leonard Bernstein's *Chichester Psalms,* my head aching from the cold winter walk to the hall and my stomach anguished from the lack of music.

If the concert had been televised, you could have turned the volume off and seen. Our conductor's body said it all: her feet rooted to the stage—heels together, toes out—her shoulders hunching ever more forward. Tension vibrated in the air around her. At a critical moment she would look up, only to see half of us in the chorus looking down. The organist squawked and stumbled. The boy soloist sang "The Lord is my shepherd" like he wished he were somewhere—anywhere—else. The conductor's gestures became larger, heavier, harder to follow. She was trying to *make* music. We gave her nothing of the kind.

An hour later, I left the hall, my soul dry, deflated. And furious, because every cell in my body vibrated with the knowledge of what it could have been.

In rehearsal I had cried at the flow of pure joy. Especially that part where the altos get the tune and the sopranos go up into the stratosphere for a crazy burbling descant that sounds like they're throwing tambourines in the air. Life is almost never that purely happy. The struggle that has been—and the pain that is to come—are almost always there, even in life's most triumphant moments. But not here. Not in the first movement of Bernstein's *Chichester Psalms.* Here is joy so pure, so present—wild, arm-flinging, grinning joy. Make a joyful noise unto the Lord. ONE-two, ONE-two, ONE-two-three. Faster. STEP-and-STEP-and-SKIP-two-three. No need to make music: You are music, and it dances you.

So why, why? We could do it, why didn't we? All sorts of rational reasons: In rehearsal we'd been accompanied by a fine pianist; the organist couldn't play the notes as written with the instrument provided here. We'd bustled into this hot, dry hall, refugees from air so cold it froze the hairs inside your nose in an instant. But still, I have performed with exhausted singers, singers suffering from stomach flu or elevation sickness, and made the air rejoice.

Maybe the question of why music does or doesn't happen is ridiculous. Maybe I should just be a good girl, learn my notes, show up at rehearsal, and hope for the best. But day after day, note after note, the possibility of music pulls me. Living music, when my voice floats out on the breath, and the sound returns from the back of the hall, illuminating the faces of the audience, tingling my skin—when all this combines to make me one with what is right and fine.

If I can understand when and why those moments happen in music, maybe I can create more of these moments in the rest of life. Life music: when choices turn out right and friendships flow, and I'm glad to be alive in this body on this earth today.

All I'm asking is how to manifest divinity, how to turn the lead of my life into gold on a more or less regular basis—as ridiculous as debating how many angels can dance on the head of a pin. Yet that debate gave birth to calculus, and the universe of mathematics was changed forever.

And besides, why should we leave the enormous questions to the Mahlers of this world, or the Einsteins? The rest of us have a right to the enormous questions, too. I just wish someone would hand me the score.

∽

WHETHER music appears or declines to appear seems magical. But magic has rules, as any reader of fairy tales knows. Music won't be made, but maybe music can be conjured, if you know how. And maybe the whole thing blows up in your face if you get the incantation wrong.

Rules. All right. Begin with the obvious. Every lesson begins with technique: the practice of honing body and mind into a voice that does your bidding—producing high notes, soft notes, legato lines—upon demand. We all need it, whether we sing classical, pop, rock, or folk. Our sounds may be different, but if we want the sound we ask for to be the sound that comes out—night after night, healthy or sick—we have to master some kind of technique. Classical singers master a sound that carries without amplification; pop singers master use of the microphone. It's all technique.

So we practice. Teaching the notes to our muscles; engraving the geography of the music onto our minds; playing with phrasing, dynamics, words, tempo—negotiating the best agreement we can between the composer's notation, our musical impulses, and our instrument's capabilities.

We work carefully, trying to get it right.

But I've seen *careful* squash music flat. Every rehearsal of *Carmina Burana,* I listened in wonder as the soprano soloist casually flung her pianissimo high D up into the rafters. It hovered there, softly shimmering, before flowing down the waterfall of a melisma. The chorus sighed, tasting pleasure. This is the moment when an innocent virgin turns to her importuning lover and says quietly, "Yes, I will." A stunning moment of delicate beauty in this piece that mostly dwells in the realm of loud—varying between triumphant, angry, and boisterous. Every single rehearsal, the soprano created this sweet rapture. But on performance night, she sang a safe, solid mezzo forte. The innocent girl she was portraying became a peasant woman. We who knew the piece mourned what had been lost.

A high pianissimo is exquisitely difficult, requiring all the support and energy of forte, with just a little less—what? air? low resonance?—so that it is focused but soft. If you pull back too much, the note can go flat or refuse to sound at all. So she played it safe and sang just a bit louder than usual. Singing a high pianissimo requires technique and much practice, but ultimately, it cannot be careful. Careful is about self-protection. Flamboyance is easy when you're singing loud, difficult but essential when you're singing soft.

The harder you practice something, the more you need to let go. Take coloratura runs, those little notes that are the reason we practice scales in singing and every other instrument. Sometimes

a run is only a few notes, but more often it consists of sixty-four
or more discrete pitches. You practice them over and over, learning the patterns so you don't have to remember each note;
singing each note staccato, then the whole phrase legato; trying
different rhythms, sometimes different keys; singing slowly at
first, then moving the metronome up tick by tick: the ditchdigging
of music.

And then, after all that controlled, careful work, you have to
abandon any sense of trying to get it right and just sing. The
greater the performance pressure the more difficult this is.

At an audition years ago, I was singing an Italian art song,
trying to prove that by God I could so too sing all those little
notes. The opening statement of the melody went fine. *Okay, here
they come, the fancy, ornamented variations.* I opened my
mouth and a phrase flew out—all by itself. Amazing. I thought
*Look at that. Goodness. So if I just do whatever I just did again,
I'm home free.* Like Lot's wife, I looked back. And, like her, I solidified. Instead of soaring, the next phrase thudded to the ground.

So I discovered that the realm of discipline is essential to
making music, but trying to get it right can destroy it. Technique
is about re-creation—practicing the phrase into reliability. Music
is creation. The well-executed crescendo must become yearning,
the skillful pianissimo transformed into awe. Maybe music happens when we add passion.

We were rehearsing Mendelssohn's oratorio *Elijah*, the opening chorus: "*Hilf, Herr.* Help, Lord." The harvest is over. There is
no food, no water. The infants cry out for bread.

We were so correct. Precisely formed German syllables. A
pretty, well-balanced Lutheran choir sound. We waited for praise
from conductor Edo de Waart.

Instead, he paused, and then this native of the Netherlands said, "You sound like the Dutch—like people who have never missed a meal. This time *sing*."

This time the choir heard the hungry children crying as we beseeched, "Lord, hear our prayer."

Passion need not mean tragic or epic; sometimes a simple word or two is enough. I was one of a chorus of teenagers in T-shirts and cutoff jeans preparing Haydn's oratorio *The Seasons* for parents' weekend at music camp. Rehearsal time was getting short. The notes were there, the theme of the fugue tossed correctly from voice part to voice part, but something was missing. "Just do it like that," the conductor told us, "but think 'mountaintop.' "

" 'Mountaintop?' " someone asked.

"Just 'mountaintop.' "

Something shifted—spirit? cheek muscles?—and sent the sound leaping into a space of delight that had not existed before.

But I have seen passion prevent music, too—at a master class given by pianist Martin Isepp for recital singers and their accompanists. The student was singing about Mary Queen of Scots with such eloquence, when her voice caught, choking on something invisible. She went on, shaken. Four bars later, she simply stopped, put her hand over her eyes, and cried. "I keep thinking about Mary, alone, in prison."

Isepp asked her to try again. She sang two notes, then choked, so he called a break. We singers murmured in the halls, sympathetic for her, grateful it wasn't us.

When we were back in our seats, Isepp said sternly, "This happens. If you love the music at all it must happen, but it should happen in the practice room." He went on, "There was a performance that Janet Baker and I did of the *Kindertotenlieder,*

Mahler's "Songs on the Death of Children," which are so sad they probably ought never to have been written. We were so close, so close to breaking down. I don't think we could have made it another two bars."

∾

Wise, full of mischief, John Brantner was a professor of psychology with a shock of white hair in a ponytail down his back, decades before men's ponytails became chic. He established the last class of his med school seminar on death and dying as a musical concert, because, he said, "There are things you can say with music that you can't say with words."

The soprano who usually sang wasn't available. I exchanged my role of auditor for performer on the condition that I could add some of my own repertoire to the Purcell, Schubert, Hindemith, and Mompou he had already programmed. I wanted to sing "My Man's Gone Now" from *Porgy and Bess*. I worked, oh, how I worked. The notes, the tone, the diction (not proper, but well-pronounced dialect), and the breath for the long wail at the end. I took long walks, imagining the woman in the opera, her terrible grief, her vision of death.

The first performance left me frightened, exhausted. "John, this one's too hard. I see him walking toward me—'old man sorrow come to keep me company.' I feel him 'whispering beside me.' I feel his breath on the back of my neck. I almost can't sing."

"Yes," said John, "it's dangerous. That's why I love watching you do it."

That's why he loved watching. Oh, yeah. Him, them, the listeners. How could I consider what makes music without considering the audience? I've sat in the audience, felt surrounded by the united exhilaration that marks a great performance. I've felt alone, too, the only stony face in a crowd of laughing, applauding people, or the only one laughing when all around me are quiet.

From the hot side of the stage lights, I've performed opera for fathers and sons, stoic, manly fellows, hungry for the next item on the PTA agenda—pizza. I've sung Gilbert and Sullivan for a boatload of people whose day on the boat had entirely too much booze and wave action.

But there are also audiences who give you more than you deserve. Two hundred singers trooped into First Baptist Church at seven o'clock that night, resplendent in our many costumes—the secular choirs in black and white, the church choirs in cream and green and shiny gold. Five choirs celebrating African-American sacred music.

The concert was taking entirely too long: intermission came after two hours. We had invited the choir directors to talk about their specialties for a few minutes. Instead, they were reveling in their lectures. Gospel, spirituals, hymns, anthems—the audience was getting quite an education.

Most of them stayed because they got to sing, too—much less tiring than sitting still. With two hundred voices filling the steeply rising seats behind the pulpit, and another thousand in front, with Sanford Moore rocking away on the piano, and the kids from Macalester College on the African drums, we made a damn joyful noise.

Sam Davis was the last conductor up. Gospel musician extraordinaire, he sent us the first call in his light tenor:

Friends don't treat me

We nodded in response

> *Like they used to*
> *Since I laid my burden down*

The audience caught on immediately. By the second verse they had joined us—melody and harmony—and were growing with confidence after each call:

> *Feel much better*
> *So much better*
> *Since I laid my burden down*

Sam's arrangement gave the altos two descending notes on the word "down." Definitely down, no doubt about it.

> *Burden down, Lord, burden down*

Then suddenly no call; the accompaniment disappeared beneath us. The audience caught its breath wondering and the choirs began slowly building on "Hallelujah." Tenors, percussive, like a trumpet fanfare. PAH, puh, puh, puh, HAH-lelujah, HAH-lelujah. Then adding sopranos. Then altos, basses, and finally piano and drums, louder, louder. Silence. Then a slow, swinging

> *Since I laid my*
> *Burden down*

A-men harmony under the word "down." The audience exploded, clapping, shouting. They wouldn't stop. After three and a half hours, they wouldn't go home. So Sam stood up and we did it all over again.

∞

A YEAR LATER the same five choirs—at the final concert of our collaboration—sang "Since I Laid My Burden Down" without Sam. He'd died from cancer the week before. The disease had been taking him even as that audience had exploded. Taking him and hurting him. I hate writing this. This second performance was different, not as exuberant, though the tenor from Sam's choir did a great job on the call.

Sam, so generous in not letting us know about his pain first time round. And in not knowing, singers and audience connected in a moment of triumph.

I'd like to say something profound and comforting about how great musicians may die, but their music goes on. I can't. There will never be a performance of "Since I Laid My Burden Down" like my first one, constructed as if it was of a tired, exhilarated audience, and those five choirs, and Sam's arrangement, and Sam.

∞

SO MUCH of what makes music sublime is out of any one performer's control. The conductor, the other performers, the temperature outside and in, and, most important of all, the audience—you on the other side of this transaction. You inconvenience yourselves with a trip to the concert hall, and make it possible to connect in that way we call music.

Beginning for Intermediates

*A*bout a year ago, I started hearing this bouncy tune in my head, two little phrases insistently repeating like some commercial jingle. I didn't know what song it was. I didn't know how I knew it. I hummed it for friends, and finally one said, "Oh, that's from Bach's *Magnificat: 'Et Exsultavit.'* "

Johann Sebastian Bach. How wonderful. My old friend. His two- and three-part inventions taught my fingers how to move independently on the piano. When I studied his fugues they seemed to me to distill the spirit of a conversation between generous people. The first voice makes a statement—clear, emphatic. A second voice replies "Yes, and," agreeing but adding some comment that makes the statement even more true. A third voice affirms, "Well, of course, and you could also consider," agreeing, amplifying, building variation upon variation. And a fourth voice and sometimes more.

The world is full of "yes, but" conversations: "What a wonderful idea. Too bad we don't have the budget for it." Or "What a wonderful adventure that would be, but I just can't. My job. My kids. Besides, I'm not the sort of person who does that sort of thing." Bach's fugues are all about "yes, and." They make me smile. When clients have been driving me particularly crazy, I slip Glenn Gould playing Bach's *Well Tempered Clavier* into my car's CD player and do, indeed, regain my temper as I drive out of the corporate parking lot.

I borrowed a couple of recordings of the *Magnificat* from the library. Second movement. Aria for second soprano. *Well, all right. "Et Exsultavit" is actually intended for my voice part.* Ordered the score. As I listened to the choral sections of the piece, my singing muscles twitched in memory. I must have sung the *Magnificat* sometime, but with so many works over so many seasons, I can't remember when.

Radio stations have programming directors who decide what songs should be aired. I hear a solo—from the audience, the chorus, on the radio, or out of a friend's CD player—and some tiny invisible programming director in the back of my brain notes, *Good song for Joan.* There the information lies, fallow and unconscious, until a good song becomes the right song for this time and place and I can't get the damn melody out of my head. The right song because it forces me to become a more skillful singer, but more important, the right song because within it lies some connection to the rest of my life, a connection that is struggling toward consciousness.

The score arrives—*"Et Exsultavit"* a small chapter in the larger work. Four pages, eight words, two and a half minutes. How difficult could that be?

A lovely twelve-bar introduction in 3/8 gets the feet tapping—not fast, not slow, like a walk one might take in the spring, a walk that has a bit more energy and bounce in it than usual because the trees are budding in that self-indulgent, flamboyant yellow-green they have this time of the year. How kind of you to admire them, and quite right you are, too. So you're at this spring-walking tempo, almost dancing because it's in three, but not skipping. Bach does not skip in church. And this little two-bar melody, an open handed, welcoming gesture, bounces up the scale:

Et exsultavit (and rejoices)

The singer answers herself with each syllable taking two notes apiece to meander toward the place where the phrase began:

Spiritus meus (my spirit)

The orchestra takes over for a bit (after all, we're in no hurry on this spring walk) and the singer has a couple more simple gestures. But then J. S. begins to play. He stretches the word *exsultavit* over five bars, spending most of the time on "ah." Ah, but what he does with that "ah." Not at all like what his contemporary Handel does in *Messiah*. Handel crafts neat little eight-note patterns. He moves a pattern down the scale and up, turns it upside down and inside out. But you can always recognize the pattern. That's what you sing—the pattern. It's too hard to think sixty-four individual pitches when they're whipping by. You just get the pattern in your voice ("just" may take hours and hours), hit the For-Unto-Us-a-Child-Is-Born switch that you have installed in your brain, pump a steady stream of air into the system, and go for it.

But J. S. is doing something quite different with *"Et Exsultavit."* He turns you into a violin—a melodic instrument with no words, and therefore no consonants to distract from pure tone. You hold the note for a bit, ornament it with a little turn, sing a fragment of a scale up, then down, hop from one note of an arpeggio to the next, put in an extra sharp or two, and you're in a different key. And all the time there is a sense of excitement building, a sense that you're getting somewhere. You're flitting all over the damn place—or at least your notes are—while underneath you, around you, the rhythmic pulse keeps up its springtime dance and the harmonies pull you with inevitable tension to finish the musical thought.

In Deo salutari meo (in God, my savior)

Another six bars to play with the "ah" in *salutari*, the phrase always moving toward "meo," *my* savior. Mary is full of herself and full of divinity and rejoicing in it all.

If the notes came faster, the singer could just flip that Baroque run switch. If slower, you could focus on each note within the phrase. But no, it's at this funny middle tempo. Two and a half minutes of quiet joy. Eighteenth-century joy, to be sure—a little restrained, a little refined—satin, velvet, whalebone stays—but still joy.

Mary is having a good time. The terror that led an angel to tell her "Fear not" is long gone. The news of her child's birth has become a welcome blessing. His gruesome death lies hidden in the future.

At first her joy infects me as I move the metronome faster tick by tick. I practice each turn—that little wiggle around a note so common in every music from Celtic to Arabic to Baroque. You have to elucidate a Bach turn in split-second notes that somehow still retain their identity as whole steps or half steps. You also have to toss it off like a turn is no big deal, just this little thing I happen to do when I'm thinking about the rest of the phrase. "Look, Ma, no hands," I want to crow as the two and a half minutes begin to fall into place.

But then I decide to sing it for this year's audition. The song becomes important, weighty. The turns limp instead of turning.

As a veteran singer with the Chorale, I will get ten minutes— a time that seems as brief as an Olympic dive—to sing a solo and then demonstrate my skills in: pronouncing foreign languages; producing different tone qualities ("Sing this phrase like Verdi opera, please. Good, now light with a straight tone"); sight singing (singing music you've never seen before, with no one playing your part); tonal memory (repeating back a series of pitches that the chorus conductor plays on the piano); and finally, singing a run or two from *Messiah,* to see how fast and clearly you can articulate. This annual process determines which works in the coming season I will be offered the opportunity to sing.

Season after season, Bach's motets, passions and the Mass in B Minor have come and gone without me. The Mass in B Minor really hurt: Bach's last choral work, the culmination of everything he had mastered in his long, prolific life. I so wanted to learn it from the inside, but for a Baroque piece, the orchestra conductor will typically request a small chorus of just 40 to 60 singers. Our chorus conductor has a roster of 200 to 250 to choose from, so we unchosen have plenty of company. This calculation comforts neither my vanity nor my passion for learning music.

I'm going to prove that I can so too sing Bach. As soon as that becomes my goal, I find myself pushing against an invisible wall, thick and glutinous. My voice feels heavy (so do I). Pitches go flat or they wobble with too much vibrato. You can't wobble Bach. Too much vibrato prevents the listener from hearing individual pitches as you sing the streams of little notes.

In memory, I hear my first singing teacher saying, "Heavy voices like ours are harder to move." It was nice of him to include me in that remark—him with his Metropolitan Opera basso. But his excuse to himself became my belief about myself, and it's hard to shake.

I practice and practice, getting worse and worse. Underneath the determined *I'm going to prove I can sing Bach* lies: *Maybe the conductor is right. Maybe I just can't*. Deep, debilitating fear.

So why put myself under this pressure? Why not find some easier song to audition with? Pigheadedness, certainly, but also because I want to perform it. When I'm preparing a song for performance, I work harder: attention to detail sharpens; I delve more deeply into the emotional content. I take it to a level far beyond the songs I sing for fun or even for lessons. A friend who holds a black belt in aikido tells me she competes for the same reason.

Besides, I know *"Et Exsultavit"* is *my* song. I just don't know how or why yet.

These moments happen—moments when fear, aspiration, possessiveness, and inevitability swirl together to extend an invitation. I'm ambling through life, peacefully going about my business, when I round the bend and come upon a burning bush. Crackling heat slaps my face, flames reach for the sky, but no smoke, no ashes. Wondrous. I don't like it. I can't imagine Moses did, either. I can't imagine he said, "Oh, boy, a burning bush giving me instructions. Wait till I tell everybody about this!" And yet he stayed to listen.

My bush fascinates, pulls toward its warmth and light. This is sacred ground. I want to flee.

"Who am I, to negotiate with Pharaoh?" asked Moses. Not an eloquent speaker, "slow of tongue," perhaps even a stutterer. I, too, am about to be asked to do something I don't think I can do.

The heat pricks my skin. I want to run. But I've learned that if I'm courageous enough to sit down and listen, I'll receive a glimpse of my spiritual curriculum.

Life's sacred assignments constitute a customized curriculum—structured and designed for each individual. I've heard friends look back and see this quite clearly. Nickie: "That was the time in my life when I had to learn how to say no. Home, work, church—they almost crushed me till I figured it out." Or Sally: "They offered me a big raise to take a job doing something I used to do really well but I hate. And then the former husband who left me eighteen hours after the ceremony turns up and wants to get married again. How did I get enrolled in a course called 'Forward or Backward: Case Studies in Decision Making'?"

Identifying the course you've been enrolled in is easy after the fact—just ask yourself what frustration kept confronting you in several areas of your life at the same time. But I want to know now, now when I'm feeling clumsy and stupid. Especially since a person can't run from the spiritual curriculum, although many try. Sure, a man can escape his creeping feeling of powerlessness—his middle-aged body aches all the time; he's passed over for promotion—by acquiring a red sports car and a young blonde. The cliché is played out too often to be dismissed. But the curriculum is patient. It will wait a decade or two, as the car ages and the young blonde matures into a woman who'd rather keep company with a peer than a protector. If powerlessness is on his curriculum, powerlessness will return.

I want to know my course assignment now. The simple act of naming it forces me to notice what's happening in my life. It also gives me a learner's perspective: Of course I'm not good at this yet—that's why it's been assigned to me.

I have friends who would say the spiritual curriculum is the will of an intentional, personal God. I have friends who would say you create the curriculum with your own energy. I'm not driven to assign causality. But I do believe the evidence of my eyes and my years. The spiritual curriculum is real.

I receive clues to my course assignment in songs that won't give up on me. You might read a poem, see a picture, hear a casual remark from a stranger that halts you in your tracks. You can't move for a moment. You're assaulted by the heat and light of a burning bush. Wonderful, terrifying, and definitely yours. Or you listen to a piece of music you've heard a hundred times before, and you hear something entirely new. At a performance of *Messiah,* perhaps, your old favorite "For Unto Us a Child Is Born" washes right over you, but you are moved to tears by "The People That Walked in Darkness Have Seen a Great Light." Maybe it's these particular singers, this orchestra. Maybe it's you.

But what about *"Et Exsultavit"*? Why that song now?

Bach was proving himself, too, when he wrote this *Magnificat* during his first year in Leipzig. Oh, it wasn't an audition. He already had the job—director of music for four Lutheran churches in town and head of the associated choir school. But the city council had decided to settle for Bach only after the famous Telemann and one other had turned the job down. He wasn't quite the bottom of the barrel—there were a few other applicants—but as far as the city fathers were concerned, Johann Sebastian Bach was definitely a B-list candidate. One Councillor Platz even said that "as the best men could not be got, [we] must make do with the mediocre."

During his first two seasons in Leipzig—1723–24 and 1724–25—J. S. composed a new cantata for every Sunday and every feast day: about sixty cantatas per year. I can think of no modern equivalent to such industry. The simple, physical act of writing out so much music is daunting—much less composing or rehearsing it. It's as if the TV show *Saturday Night Live* were to run fifty-two weeks a year, with every show the responsibility of one writer rather than a collection of staff writers and freelancers. Oh, and as if that one writer were also supposed to supervise the production of the scripts in four different venues every week.

The *Magnificat* is Mary's paean praising God, her response to her cousin's congratulations on the impending birth. The words are found in Luke 1:46–55. In the Lutheran Church of Bach's day a German *Magnificat* was typically sung every Sunday evening at Vespers. But at Christmas and during the Feast of Visitation in July, a Latin *Magnificat* was sung. Bach created this shining work for his first Christmas in Leipzig. Some seven or eight years later, he revised it, lowering the key from E-flat to D to make life easier for the trumpets, changing recorder parts to flute and making other practical adjustments. This is what we sing today.

The solo arias are unusually short for the music of this era.

No elaborate da capo—return of the first section—to stretch things out. Bach's musical simplicity expresses the spirit of the holy mother-to-be who is also a young girl.

Is this song trying to tell me something about babies? I hope not. I'm in my late forties.

I've never been pregnant. There have been times in my life when I've wanted a child, but I've never really wanted a baby. I resent it, though, when people ask "Oh, you don't like children?" No one ever asks if you like adults. I like some people and not others. I prefer those who are somewhat verbal, people I can trade ideas and stories with. I'm not crazy about crawling around getting dirty in uncomfortable positions—whether my companion is a toddler or a grown-up who expects me to enjoy digging carrots out of the mud on a November day when the weather is barely above freezing.

A year and a half ago, a man came into my life equipped with a quirky sense of humor, a slide rule collection, a motorcycle, a house in the suburbs, two daughters (aged nine and thirteen) and an assortment of Renaissance instruments, including mellifluous recorders (ranging from sopranino to bass) as well as krumm-horns and racketts—the buzzy, nasal sounds of which cause delight only in the ears of besotted early music aficionados.

The first year, I didn't sleep much. Oh, not because of passion (though there was plenty of that), but because I would wake up several times a night. Sometimes in total panic: What had I gotten myself into? Kids—people who always want more than you can give. Suburbs—leaf blowers and yard work servitude. Sometimes I awoke so happy I'm astonished I didn't emit the hum of a thousand-watt fluorescent lightbulb. But after fourteen months of moving closer, stepping nervously back, then dancing together again, I started sleeping through the night. I also started practicing at his house, since I was over there so much.

Something happens when I practice *"Et Exsultavit"* there. I thought you needed privacy to practice, a place where you alone get to hear your wrong notes. But here's the scene: Mort (electrical engineer and dad, chef and recorder player) is in the kitchen, mixing flour and other ingredients that he will submit to the aging bread machine. The machine will alternate complaining *ka chunk ka chunk* and then resting, and ultimately generate pizza dough. Rita (older daughter, oboist, and my personal consultant on young adult literature) is sitting at the kitchen counter in front of the downstairs computer. She's playing one of those games of puzzles within puzzles that intrigue her and daunt me to the point of exhaustion. Emma (star of my creation, that popular bedtime story series "Princess Emma and the Dragon") is running into the house to tell us she likes playing recorder but hates piano and wants to quit right now and why can't she, she's been taking lessons for more than a year and it isn't fair! Then she runs out to play basketball or draw chalk portraits on the driveway with the neighbor kids. Then she runs back in, just to check that we're still here, I guess. Very catlike—this need to reassure herself that all her territories are behaving themselves.

And me, I'm standing by the undersize electronic keyboard he bought to replace the piano that left years ago with his former wife. It's in the family area, divided from the kitchen, not by a wall, but by the counter Rita is sitting at. I hit a lot of wrong notes on the keyboard while I adjust to the small octaves and short keys. I apologize to Rita for all the funny noises I'm about to make and then I just sing. People are there, but paying no attention to me. Company but not an audience.

This companionable state can persist for half an hour or even an hour. That's how they seduce me, this family. But the girls are an ever-changing weather system. Tropical storms arrive without warning. Lightning flashes. Feelings are hurt. One girl thunders off to her room, Dad in tow. I'm left with the other. I try to help, contribute a more adult perspective on the situation, promote peace, soothe hurt feelings, support the downtrodden, do something, anything, useful. But mostly I end the day feeling like a powerless nincompoop, an old dishrag worn to shreds with mopping up other people's emotions, hardly the femme fatale who began a romance with this man a year and a half ago.

But during that practice hour, the right voice to sing *"Et Exsultavit"* shows up. My voice falls into a Bach groove, light, almost jazzy. All the many notes distinct but connected. I'm not trying too hard, not worrying if I can, but simply doing, simply singing this great song that I love because it's all graceful joy.

Find what works and do more of that—despite every school of vocal pedagogy in every conservatory in the world, that's really what learning to sing is about. Practical. Deeply superficial. Of course, to discover what works you have to be working.

Pay attention, the curriculum tells me. Pay attention to situations that elicit your best. Something is right.

I have fallen into middle-aged love: gorgeous and terrifying. By definition the province of those who have failed. If you have any self-awareness at all, you've acquired at least two checklists for evaluating prospective partners. Not the dating service checklists of desired physical characteristics, acceptable professions, income, and hobbies, but the important lists: (1) extremely stupid ways in which I habitually deceive myself about the other sex and (2) things about the other person that ought to make my alarm bells ring loud, while red flashing lights assault my eyes.

We met a year and a half ago, after phone calls initiated by a mutual friend. Immediate wow. (When he walked toward me and said "Joan?" I dropped the book I had been reading while waiting at the restaurant. A big, red book.) Two weeks later I forced myself to take a long slow walk and review the key checklists, looking for the presence of alarm-triggers. I found myself mumbling, "No. No. Not that either. Don't think so, but I'll keep my eyes open on that one. No. Nope. Not even that." Goodness.

A year and a half later I wake up next to his warmth with a children's song singing inside me, a song I didn't remember I remembered.

I feel, I feel, I feel like a morning star.

Well, that's a shining way to wake up, I yawn. Then hear more:

Shoe fly, don't bother me,

What's a shoe fly? Oh, yeah, it's really

Shoo, fly. Don't bother me,
Shoo, fly. Don't bother me,
For I belong to somebody.

"Et Exsultavit" and a shoe fly. What crazy assignment on the spiritual curriculum could they possibly represent? Not babies,

perhaps, but something about beginnings and rightness, and oh, yes, the possibility of joy. Ordinary, everyday joy, that fits comfortably between the pizza dough and chalk drawings on the driveway.

I seem to be enrolled in a course called "Beginnings 201: Beginning for Intermediates." I can remember at least three courses in the 100 series:

101—Beginning for Beginners. Becoming an Independent Person. Age range four and up. Learn to tie shoes and ride two-wheeler.

102—Entering the Real World. Age range: twenties. Work hard and achieve. External rewards will follow.

103—Rebuilding a Life. Age range: thirties. Experience everything falling apart. Dare to begin many new activities. Risk is minimized because life is so bad it could hardly get worse.

I may be revising history, but it seems to me that intermediate beginnings are more frightening. What if I fail? Yes, I know my resilience, that I can rebuild my life, that friends stand by me, that the sun still rises. But I also know exactly how much it hurts. Failure is not some nebulous possibility. The risks clearly delineate in my brain, even as I find myself packing up to head over to his place for the weekend.

The balm that calms fear is not love, as some would have you believe. Real love, ordinary who's-in-the-bathroom-I-need-it-now love is rarely soothing. The great anodyne for fear is laughter.

At the tail end of our first year together, we were walking into a restaurant, discussing the deal he'd negotiated for a new motorcycle and all its accoutrements. He'd bought the first one in his mid-forties. Now he was acquiring a Yamaha V-Star—a little bigger, a little more powerful than the old one—so we could tour more comfortably.

I offered to pick up the tab for the passenger seat back and the saddle bags, since these were directly related to my participation. He turned me down. "Okay, but why?" I asked. I expected him to say something like "It's my bike." Or to point out that he has a salaried job and I freelance.

Instead, he paused, a tight look on his face. "I just don't want you spending money on this. I'm not sure how long we're going to be together." Fear rose through me, gripping my stomach, heating my face, physical as the hot flash I'd had earlier that day, my first.

"Well, how about I pay for lunch?" I suggested. "The length of the commitment is less."

A week later, we had one of those days when minds run on parallel tracks. He had bought the bike and was pondering what to name it. The girls were clamoring for "Barney," because the bike is purple like the cuddly dinosaur on TV. Barney in black leather, a fine image, but not, perhaps, quite consonant with the biker aesthetic. I was pondering that first hot flash, bothered more by the loss of connection between my body and the real world than by aging. It had felt as if someone had abruptly turned the heat in the room to a hundred degrees, not as if there were something happening inside me. Disconcerting.

We weren't ignoring each other, just a bit distracted. We'd talk about the bike, then each drift away, then talk about female temperature fluctuations, then drift into our own thoughts again. Suddenly, "That's it!" he voiced his eureka, "We'll call it Flash!"

He wasn't able to say "I love you" yet—that would come

months later—but he named the symbol of his middle age after this symptom of mine. Not so fragile, this relationship, perhaps. Not so scary either.

J. S. is with me, I believe, as I begin Beginning for Intermediates. He knows all about starting over. By the time he died, in 1750, sixty-five years old and blind, his music had fallen into disfavor with the fashionable world. His last great works—the Mass in B Minor, *A Musical Offering, The Art of Fugue*—all were dismissed as old fashioned, conservative. His music was rarely performed, even in the St. Thomas Church of Leipzig, the recipient of so much of his musical bounty. Music was moving on toward Mozart and Haydn.

A few disciples in Berlin persisted in playing Bach for his small remaining audience. They preserved most of the original manuscripts that have survived. One Baron van Swieten carried the torch to Vienna. During the 1780s, Bach's music was performed at the baron's house, where both Mozart and Haydn heard it. As the eighteenth century moved into the nineteenth, some German Romantics were attracted to Bach as part of a back-to-our-roots movement in German history and religion. But it took Mendelssohn conducting a performance of the *St. Matthew Passion* in 1829 to transform "the revival from a cult of intellectuals into a popular movement," according to *The New Grove Dictionary of Music and Musicians*.

A similar resurrection took place among music historians and performers in England. A century after Bach's death, the English founded their Bach Society, dedicated to the collection and promotion of his works. The Germans formed the *Bachgesellschaft*, which was to spend the next fifty years publishing scores of all

Bach's works. Not bad for a guy whose music was condemned by a contemporary for its "turgid and confused style."

"Et Exsultavit" dwells about as far from turgid and confused as I can imagine. It calls me.

So often, an invitation from the spiritual curriculum comes wrapped in fear, fear and a peculiar sense of inevitability. Excitement stirs within you, and a touch of joy. You, who know entirely too well what you are risking, are about to begin.

Besides, in another few decades the 300-level course—Beginning for the Advanced Life Practitioner—is bound to show up. I may as well complete the prerequisites.

Will I sing *"Et Exsultavit"* better at the audition because it's part of my spiritual coursework? Probably. The deeper I delve into this song, the more it becomes my friend. Will I be invited to sing Bach choral works in the future? Maybe. It depends so much on what others sing, and how well. And what pieces the orchestras perform. And how large a chorus the orchestra conductors request. And a handful of other variables I have no more control over than a hot flash. Will Mort lift me up on the back of his white charger (or purple motorcycle) as we gallop (or vroom) off into the sunset? Occasionally. Will the kids delight and drive me crazy? Absolutely.

But other than that, I can't predict endings. I'm enrolled in a course on beginning. I can approach my curriculum with open heart and mind. I can work with passion and discipline; choose to struggle less and laugh more. And, of course, I will sing.

Suggested Listening

What follows is a list (by chapter) of my favorite recordings of some of the music discussed in this book. I have not attempted to name the definitive recordings of larger works: There are good directories available in both music stores and online that can provide you with reviews from music experts and lay people. Nor have I attempted to ensure that all recordings are still available for purchase, since I have found many treasures in the public library. So, here are a few recordings I enjoy and you might, too.

Harmonium and Tessitura

Harmonium by John Adams. Edo De Waart conducting the San Francisco Symphony Chorus and Symphony Orchestra BMG/ECM 21277

Creativity's Compost

"The Man I Love" by George Gershwin. One of the great Gershwin albums is *Naughty Baby: Maureen McGovern Sings Gershwin*, Sony/Columbia. Jazzy artistry from McGovern and great collaboration from her combo.

Quartet Making

Precious Friend, Arlo Guthrie and Pete Seeger. I have been priviledged to see this great musical friendship in concert several times. I wore out my copy of the cassettes of this live recording and had to buy it on CD. Great music for all ages to sing along to. Warner Bros.

"The Monk and His Cat" from *Hermit Songs* by Samuel Barber. There are two recordings of *Hermit Songs* that I recommend:

1. Leontyne Price sings with all the colors and moods of her great voice. Samuel Barber accompanies, and it's always a treat to hear the composer perform: Other great performances of Barber's music on this CD are Eleanor Steber, Dietrich Fischer-Dieskau, and Martina Arroyo. *Samuel Barber:*

222   How Can We Keep from Singing

Knoxville Summer of 1915, Dover Beach, Hermit Songs, Andromache's Farewell, Sony Masterworks Portrait, MPK 46727

2. If Price's old-fashioned, operatic pronunciation of English annoys you (she rolls her "r"s), turn to Cheryl Studer's recording with John Browning at the piano. *Secrets of the Old: Complete Songs of Samuel Barber,* Deutsche Grammophon 435 867-2

Practice for a Singing Life

"Chanson Bohème" ("Gypsy Song") from *Carmen* by Georges Bizet. Julia Migenes-Johnson as Carmen. Orchestre National de France, Choeurs et Maitrise de Radio France, Lorin Maazel Conducting. Wea/Atlantic Erato 45207 (the complete opera) or 45209 (excerpts). Migenes-Johnson had a lot of music theater experience when she recorded this in 1982. I love the way it shows up in this recording. She starts the song at a slow sizzle and proceeds to become wilder and wilder, verse after verse.

Conductor Watching

Robert Shaw recorded all three composers' versions of the *Stabat Mater* on two different recordings:

1. *Stabat Mater: Szymanowski & Poulenc.* Robert Shaw, Atlanta Symphony Orchestra & Chorus, Telarc 80362CD

2. *Verdi: Quattro Pezzi Sacri.* Robert Shaw, Atlanta Symphony Orchestra & Chorus, Telarc 80254CD

Balm in Gilead

"Sometimes I Feel Like a Motherless Child," sung by Odetta. Her rich, smokey voice is the one in hear inside my head when I need this song. *The Essential Odetta* Vanguard CD and cassette

"Spirituals in Concert." There is a CD of the televised Carnegie Hall concert that I refer to, but I prefer the videotape. It's available in many libraries. Kathleen Battle and Jessye Norman sing; James Levine conducts the unidentified chorus and orchestra. You can catch a glimpse of Sylvia Olden Lee accompanying her "girls" on the piano in "Scandalize My Name." Deutsche Grammophon 072 249-3

Teach Your Children Well

"Caro mio ben." Cecilia Bartoli has made a marvelous recording of the Italian art songs that classical singers begin their studies with. Bartoli shows just how luminous music this can be: *If You Love Me,* Uni/London Classics 36267

Beginning for Intermediates

"Et Exsultavit" from the Bach *Magnificat.* I love the cleanliness of the Shaw recording. He achieves an elegant middle ground between the emotional heaviness of previous generations and the wispy lightness of some of the period music recordings. Penelope Jensen's rendition of *"Et Exsultavit"* is forthright and warm. On the same recording, Jensen and the young Dawn Upshaw give us a delicious duet (*"Laudamus Te"*) in the Vivaldi *Gloria.* Vivaldi *Gloria*, Bach *Magnificat.* Robert Shaw, Atlanta Symphony Orchestra & Chorus. Telarc 80194CD